THE NFT EQUATION

HOW TO NAVIGATE & PROFIT IN THE NFT SPACE AS A BEGINNER, INVESTOR, OR ARTIST

JARED T. ROSS

© **Copyright 2021 - All rights reserved.**

The content contained within this book may not be reproduced, duplicated, or transmitted without direct written permission from the author or the publisher.

Under no circumstances will any blame or legal responsibility be held against the publisher, or author, for any damages, reparation, or monetary loss due to the information contained within this book, either directly or indirectly.

Legal Notice:

This book is copyright protected. It is only for personal use. You cannot amend, distribute, sell, use, quote, or paraphrase any part, or the content within this book, without the author or publisher's permission.

Disclaimer Notice:

Please note that the information contained within this document is for educational and entertainment purposes only. All effort has been executed to present accurate, up-to-date, reliable, complete information. No warranties of any kind are declared or implied. Readers acknowledge that the author is not rendering legal, financial, medical, or professional advice. The content within this book has been derived from various sources. Please consult a licensed professional before attempting any techniques outlined in this book.

By reading this document, the reader agrees that under no circumstances is the author responsible for any losses, direct or indirect, that are incurred due to the use of the information in this document, including, but not limited to, errors, omissions, or inaccuracies.

CONTENTS

Introduction — 7

1. WHAT IS AN NFT (NFT & BLOCKCHAIN FUNDAMENTALS) — 17
   The Blockchain Explained — 18
   Non-Fungible Tokens (NFTs) Explained — 21
   A Peek Inside My NFT Wallet — 24

2. WHY SKEPTICS HATE NFTS (BUT ACTUALLY SHOULDN'T) — 35
   I Can Just Screenshot Them — 36
   Greater Fool Theory — 39
   Art Theft — 40
   The Rich Get Richer — 41
   NFTs Are a Scam — 43
   NFTs Are a Bubble — 44
   Unnecessary Decentralization — 44

3. WHY NFTS HAVE VALUE — 49
   Avatar/Character Style & Profile Pictures (PFP) — 57
   Arts & Media — 59
   Digital Collectibles — 60
   Gaming — 61
   Virtual Land — 65
   Memberships, Access, Tickets — 67
   Alternative Payment Methods — 68
   Decentralized Autonomous Organizations (DAOs) — 69

4. THE EXACT STEPS TO GET STARTED 75
   INVESTING OR CREATING
   Preliminary Steps 76
   Step 1 - Setting Up Your Wallet 77
   Step 2 - Acquiring Cryptocurrency 85
   Step 3 - Connecting To An NFT 93
   Marketplace

5. HOW TO BUY YOUR FIRST NFT 97
   Step 1 - Wallet & Opensea Set Up 98
   Step 2 - Determine Your Objective & 98
   Select an NFT
   Step 3 - Click the Buy Now Button 101
   Alternate Step 3 - Making an Offer 106
   Step 4 - Locating Your NFT 110

6. HOW TO CREATE YOUR FIRST NFT WITH 113
   NO TECHNICAL SKILLS
   Creating / Minting an NFT on Rarible 114
   Creating / Minting an NFT on Opensea 122
   Lazy Minting vs Custom Smart Contracts 127

7. THE INVESTOR'S APPROACH 131
   Finding NFT Projects 133
   Projects To Avoid 136
   Analyzing New Project Fundamentals 144
   Analyzing Established Project 158
   Fundamentals

8. TOP NFT FLIPPING STRATEGIES 169
   Pre-Reveal Flipping 169
   Momentum Flipping 178
   Long Term / Blue Chip Flipping 182

9. THE CREATOR'S APPROACH ... 189
   Fundamentals for NFT Creators ... 189
   NFTs For Artists ... 193
   NFTs For Business Owners ... 195
   NFTs For The Opportunists ... 198

10. METAVERSE/NFT SAFETY & SECURITY ... 199
   Most Common Scams ... 200
   Security Strategies ... 206

   Conclusion ... 211
   Special Thanks ... 215
   References ... 217

INTRODUCTION

I was too young to take advantage of the birth of the internet and, if you're like me, you've thought to yourself, "I wonder how my life would be different if I were an early adopter or innovator of the Internet & dot com boom....." I always felt like I was out of luck having missed that opportunity.

Until now.

I believe that ignoring NFTs and the metaverse will be one of the most expensive decisions you could make this decade. Moreover, I think the metaverse and NFTs offer an opportunity as big as the internet in its infancy. But why does that matter, and how exactly are you supposed to take advantage of this confusing space if no one can even articulate what an NFT actually is?

Those were my thoughts exactly when I first started hearing all the buzz about these "non-fungible tokens" (NFTs) and how the industry has blown up to be worth over **$40 billion** in seemingly no time (Versprille, 2022). I started out skeptical and confused, and when I began my attempts at trying to wrap my mind around how it makes any sense to be buying JPEGS for obscene amounts of money, I discovered that most people involved in the space had little to no clue of what they were actually engaged in or were just terrible at explaining it to me.

In fact, you've likely been lied to about the NFT space. People may have put the idea in your head that NFTs are just digital art, scams, worthless, or just for fun. These ideas are simply untrue, and in this book, I'll prove it.

I spent many months smelling this NFT opportunity without a clear path to take advantage of it myself because it was all so confusing. Fortunately, I'm a gifted learner and able to take in, synthesize and simplify information. As I began to understand the NFT space more intimately, I quickly found that I am also a gifted teacher who was one of the few able to put NFTs in plain English and give clear guidance to thousands of people on getting started themselves. I've condensed what I've learned and what I teach into the NFT Equation. The NFT Equation is the framework I've used to go from skeptical and confused to empowered and obsessed in the NFT space, and I believe it will do the same for you!

Although I've been involved in cryptocurrency since late 2017 and therefore had some context and understanding of NFTs (since they're on the blockchain as well), it wasn't until early 2021 that I dove into NFTs. At the time, I was a senior at the University of San Francisco about to graduate with honors the following semester with a Bachelor's in Entrepreneurship & Innovation.

Despite building an immaculate reputation at the institution; including joining the Alumni Board of Directors (yes, as an undergrad), consistently being on the dean's list, organizing creative projects on campus, creating on-campus jobs, holding leadership workshops, working closely with admin on campus initiatives and student retention...I decided to retire (drop out) from the University.

As you can imagine, this was an incredibly difficult decision to make. In the 3+ years I spent at the University, I created so many incredible relationships with faculty and students, enhanced my professional skills, and grew as a person and student. Especially being so close to graduation, many people believed that I wasted all the time I already spent there. That couldn't be further from the truth.

I went to college because I had a massive scholarship and I wanted the experience, networking, and opportunities that came from it. I got exactly what I came for and I am thoroughly satisfied with my overall experience (I would do it all over again). In fact, I loved my school and still donate time and money to enhance the community there.

Although attending the University of San Francisco was an all around incredible experience, the opportunities I was finding and creating in the world of entrepreneurship demanded I make a sacrifice. Ultimately, it came down to asking myself how my time would best be utilized: earning a degree I never intended to utilize or focusing full-time on building a community and business of my own.

Fortunately, the faith and confidence I have myself gave me the courage to make the jump in spite of the paralyzing fear that came with the idea of dropping out. So, just one semester before graduating, I decided to retire from University and focus on entrepreneurship and building my personal brand. Again, NFTs and the metaverse were not the only reason I decided to drop out, but they ended up being what I became obsessive about mastering.

Fast forward just seven short months later, after building an online audience and earning tens of thousands in the NFT space after going full time; I was back at the University of San Francisco as a guest lecturer to teach students about NFTs and the Metaverse. Using the relationships I built at the school, I was fortunate enough to be invited back to my old University to teach the NFT Equation course material! So yes, what you'll read in this book and experience inside the course this book is based on, has been taught at the University level multiple times.

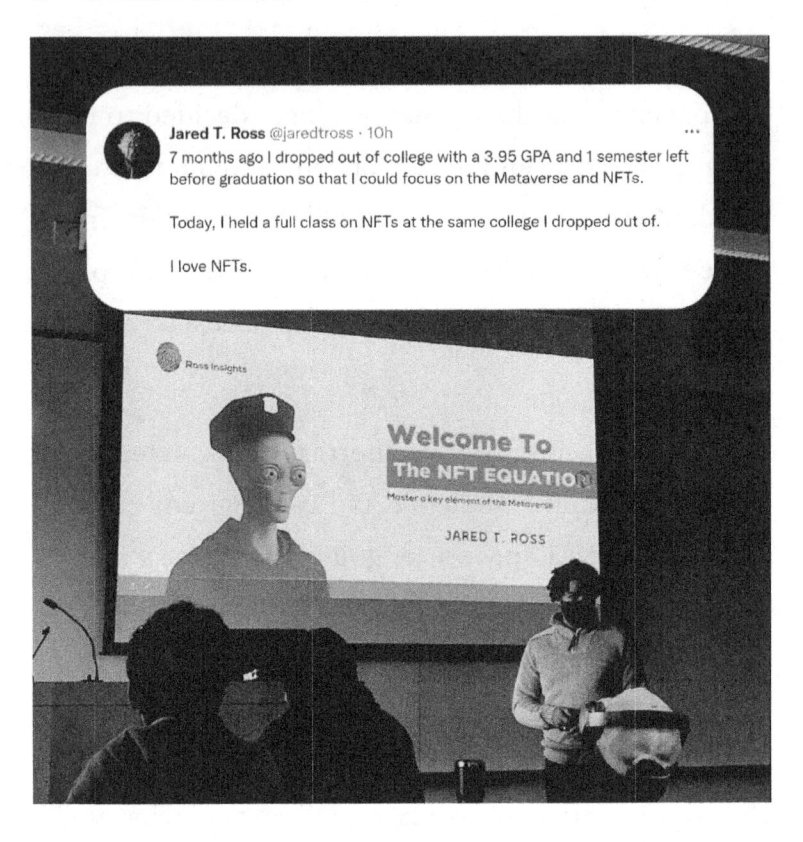

In fact, it went so well that I was even asked to come back and teach again the following semester.

> Thanks for sharing Jared! Those companies look pretty interesting... lots more to think about in this space. I look forward to continuing the conversation.
>
> Also I was wondering... would you be interested in coming back next semester to do the same session in my class? I'm only teaching one section, so it would be a little easier on your schedule, and it would likely occur in mid to late April on a Tuesday or Thursday afternoon.
>
> Thanks,

I share all this to say that I know both what I'm talking about and how to talk about it in a way that makes sense for people without context or experience in the space. That said, there will be many times I'll address something in this book that won't make sense until you execute. The NFT space is incredibly hands-on, and the best education will come from doing. If you encounter these moments where something doesn't quite register, I ask that you be patient with yourself and with me.

So, before we dive into the education piece, let me provide some context on what exactly the NFT Equation is. In short, The NFT Equation is a framework for approaching and navigating the NFT space successfully, both from the creator side and the investor side. Originally designed and built into a complete, highly structured, and organized video course that's constantly evolving and updated in real-time, I'm condensing some of the key course modules into this book that you're reading now. The course has hundreds of students already enrolled, with more getting in daily. You can learn more about the course and hear student testimonials by visiting www.nftequation.com/enroll. At the end of this book, I'll also provide a juicy discount for those interested in furthering their education!

Anyway, you are getting a taste of the course right here inside this book at a fraction of the cost. I'm writing this book in an effort to make the course material more affordable and more digestible for as many people as possible. I'm excited to walk you through what an NFT is, how to get started buying or creating them, why NFTs have value in the first place, flipping NFTs, keeping yourself safe, and much more!

I have a saying that "the future moves faster." This captures the reality that the rate of innovation is increasing each year, and it's becoming more challenging to keep up with it. This book aims to give you the information you need to be better prepared to keep up with the future. Let's get into it!

1
WHAT IS AN NFT (NFT & BLOCKCHAIN FUNDAMENTALS)

We'll start by making sure you have a solid understanding of NFT and blockchain fundamentals. If that sounds intimidating, take a breath because what you'll notice throughout this book is that I have a gift of simplifying this entire world you're about to enter.

This chapter is likely to be the least "sexy" part of the book because it's mostly about definitions and building some context for those who are totally foreign to the blockchain world. Simultaneously, this will be one of the most essential chapters because of the background it gives you. Most people are jumping into NFTs without a clue in the world what an NFT actually is. It may work out for them in the short term, but without these fundamental understandings, they'll eventually miss opportunities or put themselves at tremendous risk due to a lack of knowledge.

Those that skip this chapter will be rolling the dice on their success in the NFT space, but not you. So, let's get into it by first defining what a "blockchain" actually is.

THE BLOCKCHAIN EXPLAINED

Keep in mind that this book is designed to be welcoming and easy to understand for beginners. There are many technical details we could dive into that would enhance your understanding, but I'll focus on the purpose of the book and keep it as non-technical as possible.

Put simply; a "blockchain" is a digital, globally distributed, public ledger, or database, that allows anyone connected to the internet to view all the transactions that have ever happened on that particular blockchain and the wallets associated with each transaction.

Now you may be thinking: "Okay, Jared, but why can't we just have a globally shared Google Spreadsheet essentially?"

And the answer lies in the WAY data is stored, processed, and verified as true and accurate on the blockchain compared to a typical database.

As explained by Investopedia, "One key difference between a typical database and a blockchain is how the data is structured. A blockchain collects information together in groups, known as blocks, that hold sets of information. Blocks have certain storage capacities and, when filled, are closed and linked to the previously filled block, forming a chain of data known as the blockchain. All new information that follows that freshly added block is compiled into a newly formed block that will then also be added to the chain once filled.

A database usually structures its data into tables, whereas a blockchain, like its name implies, structures its data into chunks (blocks) that are strung together. This data structure inherently makes an irreversible timeline of data when implemented in a decentralized nature. When a block is filled, it is set in stone and becomes a part of this timeline. Each block in the chain is given an exact timestamp when it is added to the chain." (Hayes, 2022)

But more than that, the data on the blockchain is secured and verified as true using a type of encryption called cryptography. Avoiding the more technical explanation of cryptography, it's simply a type of encryption that helps protect and confirm data. Once a transaction (data) is successfully verified or confirmed, it is put on the blockchain and theoretically immutable (unchangeable).

To summarize, the blockchain is a public, digital record of transactions that everyone can see, and trust is true and accurate.

Blockchains were theorized as a cryptographically secured chain of blocks (chunks of data) as early as the 1980s & 1990s by scientists like Stuart Haber and Scott Stornetta, with many other scientists publishing their own ideas and theorizing utilizing the concept. The first actual application of blockchain technology as a peer-to-peer network was in 2009 with the introduction of the Bitcoin cryptocurrency.

Blockchains are theoretically useful for providing a trustless financial system, faster transactions than traditional banking, more direct control over one's funds, and more transparency over transactions as a whole. Due to the blockchain's distributed and immutable nature, this technology helps provide proof of ownership over a variety of assets and proof of origin/authenticity.

It's important to note that there are multiple blockchains. Bitcoin has its own, Ethereum has its own, Solana has its own, and there are plenty others out there, but the vast majority of this book will focus on Ethereum-based NFTs. Keep in mind that not all blockchains are created equal or even perform in the idealistic way blockchain advocates proclaim. Nonetheless, most of what you learn will also apply to NFTs on other blockchains.

We won't spend much more time diving into the background and history of the blockchain because I don't believe it's vital to you getting your start in the NFT space. Still, it's helpful to know a bit nonetheless, and you'll certainly be learning more as you dive deeper into NFTs.

NON-FUNGIBLE TOKENS (NFTS) EXPLAINED

Now to address the big question everyone has: "what the hell is an NFT anyways?"

If you're like me, you wanted to slap people upside the head when you asked that, and they responded, "it's a non-fungible token." I know that when I was first getting started, it was very frustrating trying to find a simple and accurate definition or explanation of NFTs, and when people responded by telling me what the acronym stood for, it was incredibly unhelpful!

We'll address the acronym first, but afterward, I promise you that I'll provide one of the easiest to understand definitions of NFTs you've ever heard.

NFT does, indeed, stand for "non-fungible token," but what does that even mean? An asset that is non-fungible means it cannot be easily replaced for something else because it's unique. For example, plots of land would be considered non-fungible because each plot has its own unique properties that won't be exactly the same as another plot.

On the other hand, something that is fungible can easily be swapped without compromising any essential qualities or traits. An excellent example of a fungible asset would be two gold bars of equal weight and purity. Two people can easily swap these without compromising or missing out on anything since they're getting an exactly equivalent asset in return.

THE NFT EQUATION 23

Now, I've been exactly where you are right at this moment...someone told me that NFT means non-fungible token and then explained non-fungible vs fungible, and you **still** don't know what an NFT really is.

Rest assured, I've been there, and I know that's likely not enough to truly wrap your mind around this concept. An easier way of looking at NFT is as a uniquely identifiable digital asset whose ownership can be proven and verified on the blockchain. These digital assets typically take the form of a photo, GIF, or video. While these are often simply art pieces, they can also be visual representations of products and services.

Notice what I just said, NFTs are **not** digital art. They can be, but fundamentally they are not, in and of themselves, simply digital art. Like the blockchain, NFTs at their core offer proof of authenticity, proof of ownership, and immutability. Now think, what industries in the world might be able to benefit from proof of ownership, proof of authenticity, and immutability?

The answer is just about every industry on the planet. Although it is what we're used to seeing so far in NFTs' infancy, we must remove this idea that NFTs are just fun little art projects. And don't worry, in chapter 2, I'll tear apart the idea that you own an NFT just by screenshotting it.

While NFTs really caught the public's eye in 2021 and blew the industry up to be worth billions of dollars, the first NFT ever, titled "Quantum," was created back in 2014 by Kevin McCoy. Even the popular Cryptopunks selling for millions nowadays were created (and given away for free, by the way) back in 2017. I bring up this brief history just to illustrate that these didn't just pop up in 2020 or 2021. They've been here for years, and people have been experimenting with them and trying to find their true value and utility.

Even at this point, the true concept of NFTs may still be a little hazy, so when I am explaining them to people, I always like to drive the point home by showing them some of the NFTs I own inside my wallet and breaking down why they're valuable to me.

So, let's take a look.

A PEEK INSIDE MY NFT WALLET

After hearing my simplified definition of an NFT (a uniquely identifiable digital asset whose ownership can be proven and verified on the blockchain), many people are still confused until I showcase some concrete examples of NFTs that I currently own.

First up, we'll visit the Enigma Economy project.

The founding team launched an NFT project with thousands of varied NFTs with this art style, and they are using the funds raised from that launch to create a physical crypto mining operation. Let's recall what we learned about the blockchain earlier and how its cryptography is what helps it be verifiably true and immutable. The process of confirming a submitted transaction as true and accurate requires computers with enough computational power to solve incredibly complex mathematical equations that humans can't solve. Once multiple computers successfully solve a transaction and all come to the same conclusion or answer, the blockchain then knows to accept it and place it in the records as verified and true. This process of solving these transactions is called "mining." Each time a computer successfully solves a transaction, the associated wallet will be rewarded with a small amount of cryptocurrency.

If you do some research on google and look up "crypto mining facilities," what you'll notice is that cryptomining could be done on an incredibly small scale, like just setting up an extra computer rig at home. Or as extensive as buying property and filling it with thousands of machines dedicated to mining and collecting those mining rewards.

The Enigma Economy project falls into the latter. They're setting up a warehouse and purchasing thousands of GPUs (computers that will be solving the transactions) to set up in their facility that they are paying for using the funds from the launch. In this context, the NFTs functioned as a crowdfunding platform for the company. So, why did people even want to buy into this project and help it get going?

The cool part about this project is that anyone who owns one of the NFTs from the project will be entitled to a certain percentage of the mined cryptocurrency this facility earns. Put simply, by holding one of these NFTs (I own four at the time of this writing), I'll be able to earn passive crypto income without doing anything myself.

Now look back at the artwork (visual element) of this NFT project. The truth is...I don't even *like* the artwork! It doesn't matter in the slightest. Recall that NFTs will typically have some type of visual component to add some personality and capture interest in the first place. Still, the artwork is mostly irrelevant when an NFT's primary value is the utility.

I bought into this project for the utility, or ownership benefit, of earning passive income just by holding onto it. The visual element (artwork) could have literally been a black square and I would've purchased it.

We'll dive into this deeper in the next chapter, but people like to make fun of NFTs and say, "I can just screenshot it and now I have your NFT." The Enigma Economy is a great illustration of why people who say that have no understanding of NFTs. People can screenshot this NFT all they want, but they won't receive the passive income that comes with actually owning it because this NFT is stored inside a cryptocurrency wallet and, because it's all on the blockchain, the founding team can see which wallets own the NFTs, and they simply send the free crypto to those wallets.

Now, let's consider the CityDAO Citizen NFT pictured below.

The team behind this project has purchased physical real estate in the state of Wyoming, intending to build a city and connect it to the blockchain by allowing NFT holders the right to vote on how the land will be used and divided up into parcels. This business structure called a decentralized autonomous organization, or DAO, is something we'll dive into in a future chapter. This project is another instance of the artwork being completely irrelevant to my decision to buy it because I bought for the utility.

This project has even caught the attention of the co-founder of the Ethereum cryptocurrency, Vitalik Buterin, when he featured it on his blog post about the future of NFTs and the blockchain, which you can find at https://vitalik.ca/general/2021/10/31/cities.html.

Next up is the Jadu hoverboard brought to you by a legit augmented reality (AR) company with huge backing and a genius team. Owning one of these allows me to use my hoverboard in their AR app to play with other compatible NFT avatars that can ride the board and participate in AR challenges and scavenger hunts to win free NFTs.

THE NFT EQUATION   31

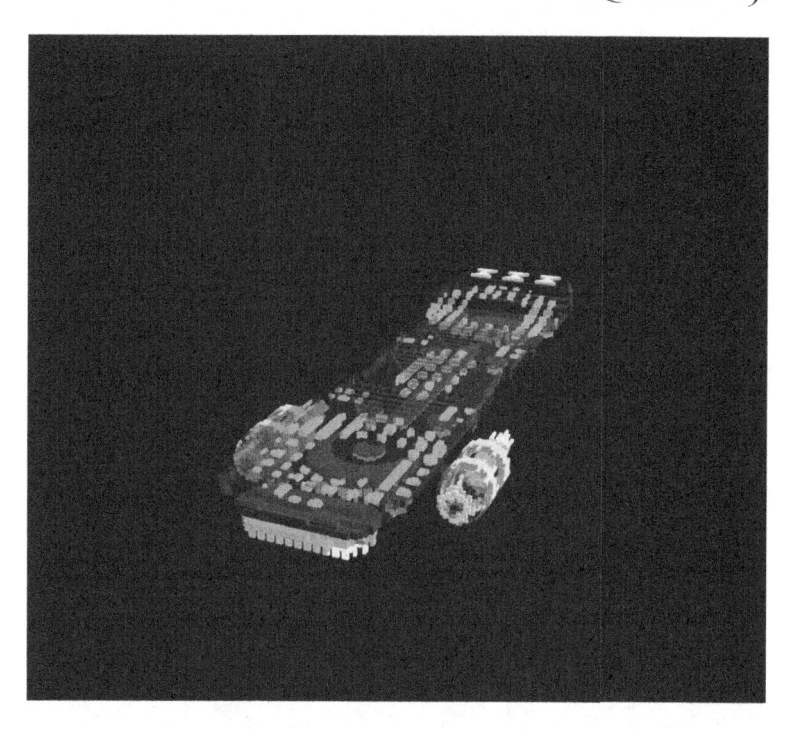

Finally, we have jaredtross.eth, which is a domain name just like jaredtross.com, but it's on the blockchain, which allows me to build a decentralized website on it (uncensorable) and use the address to accept crypto payments instead of that long, complicated string of numbers and letters that are your typical crypto addresses (0x8B9003895229E4025Ee62F977d3ac11C7D7fA799 for example). In short, it helps with branding and identity in the web 3 and blockchain worlds.

jaredtross.eth

*The background image of this domain name is actually another NFT that I own, and I just connected the two of them.

I explain all this to say: the value of an NFT is not in the ability to look at them, but in everything else that comes with true ownership. The further you read into this book, the more apparent this will become, and, by the end, you just may find yourself impassioned with this whole world and the opportunity it presents.

By the way, you can further explore my wallets (I have multiple) by visiting the NFT marketplace Opensea and simply searching my name all as one word, "jaredtross," and you'll find two of my wallets with NFTs inside.

At this point, you should now have some context and a more thorough understanding of the world you are entering by getting into NFTs. You will still be confused at times, but I encourage you to continue and learn more despite the frustrations. And honestly, the proper understanding will only come as you begin executing and putting into practice what you learn throughout this book.

In this next chapter, I will address some of the most popular reasons people decide to hate NFTs and why most of them really stem from a fundamental lack of understanding instead of legitimate concerns.

2

WHY SKEPTICS HATE NFTS (BUT ACTUALLY SHOULDN'T)

For some reason, the tension between those for NFTs and those against them is akin to the tension between angry vegans and meat-eaters. Oftentimes with attacks on character and morale from the anti-NFT camp and attacks on intellect, typically from the pro-NFT camp. One thing is clear about the NFT space: if you even know it exists, you either hate NFTs with a burning passion or love them with that same intensity. And then there's a microscopic segment of the population who are somewhere in the middle where they know that NFTs exist but aren't sure where they stand yet.

This book is designed for that TINY sliver of people who are vaguely conscious of what an NFT is and somewhat interested in them but just need that guidance to get started and find out why NFTs are such an enjoyable industry to be a part of.

While this small segment is my focus, I will, of course, need to address the skeptics and haters of NFTs. Hopefully, when you encounter the inevitable ostracism from friends and family who find out you've dared to even learn about NFTs, you'll be able to kindly and gracefully dismantle their main objectives related to NFTs.

Like the angry vegan trying to make a point, it's not uncommon for NFT advocates to address their adversaries with a condescending tone that belittles and prevents proper communication of ideas. Therefore, although I'm likely to use some sarcasm, I hope to field opponents' objections to NFTs with mutual respect in an effort to improve communication. Let us begin.

I CAN JUST SCREENSHOT THEM

Once again, I remind you that the value of NFTs is not in being able to literally see them but in the ownership benefits *behind* them. At the most basic level, the ownership benefit all NFTs possess is the ability to resell it. You can't go and resell a screenshot of an original piece (unless you want to violate copyright laws).

Critics tease NFT owners saying, "I just screenshotted it," thinking they now own the NFT. If they paused and thought it through rationally, they'd realize how stupid they sound (respectfully).

Let's consider physical art for a moment. Famed painter Jean-Michel Basquiat had one of his paintings sell for over $110 Million a few years ago (post mortem). If you google "Jean-Michel Basquiat $100 million," you'll easily be able to find pictures of the artwork. You can screenshot the image or print it out if you like; it has absolutely ZERO impact on the value of the piece itself. Fundamentally, we all know this, but for whatever reason, people seem to think it doesn't apply to digital assets.

Go take a screenshot of your bank account balance right after a payday and let me know if you still have the same amount of money in there after spending some of it since you still have the screenshot. As silly as that sounds, that's what people are suggesting when they think they own an NFT by screenshotting it.

Being able to view a digital or physical asset at your leisure does not equate to ownership or possession.

Still not convinced?

Let's recall the NFTs of mine from the last chapter. Take the Enigma Economy NFT, for instance. I invite anyone who uses this "screenshot" argument to look up that project on Opensea and screenshot every single one of them (there's over 8,000). If that screenshot means ownership, the screenshotter should receive those passive income rewards for years to come.

Hint: they won't receive anything.

What about the CityDAO Citizen NFT project? Screenshot away, then go ahead and look that project up on the voting platform called Snapshot.org. On that site, you'll need to connect your crypto wallet that contains the NFT, and then you'll be able to vote on any decisions the company is considering at the moment. Once again, a screenshot means absolutely nothing in this case either.

As NFT owners, we actually WANT people to screenshot and share the NFTs we own! The attention brings more notoriety (and hopefully more demand) to our assets. We don't have to hide them from the world!

GREATER FOOL THEORY

I'll be honest, the Greater Fool Theory is definitely applicable to the NFT space right now, but I don't think it's necessarily a fundamental component of it in the long run. As defined by Hartford Funds, "The Greater Fool Theory is the idea that, during a market bubble, one can make money by buying overvalued assets and selling them for a profit later, because it will always be possible to find someone who is willing to pay a higher price. An investor who subscribes to the Greater Fool Theory will buy potentially overvalued assets without any regard for their fundamental value. This speculative approach is predicated on the belief that you can make money by gambling on future asset prices and that you will always be able to find a "greater fool" who will be willing to pay more than you did. Unfortunately, when the bubble eventually bursts (which it always does), there is a large sell-off that causes a rapid decline in the asset values. During the sell-off, you can lose a great deal of money if you are the one left holding the asset and cannot find a buyer." (Bogan, 2021).

NFT Skeptics won't hear me argue much with them on this aspect. Still, I will point out that this certainly isn't unique to the NFT market, so if this alone is enough to make you despise NFTs...you might also want to point your hatred to at least a dozen other markets, including real estate and the stock market. I'd also point out that once we experience this bubble burst, I think we'll find far more people interested in projects with solid and value-adding fundamentals rather than all the low-quality NFT projects we see today.

ART THEFT

Another big complaint about NFTs is that they hurt artists more than help empower them. A chief culprit of the damage NFTs can cause to artists is the rampant art theft. This is a legitimate gripe with NFTs that I believe will become less prevalent as the space grows and regulation is implemented.

As of now, anyone could find an artist's work online and turn it into an NFT to sell it as if it was their own. Is it a violation of copyright regulation? Of course, it is, but given the semi-anonymous nature of the blockchain and the allure of the NFT space and digital art right now, most of these art thieves don't really care. Many NFT advocates would tell artists that they should've jumped on the NFT wagon sooner, and then it would be easier for people to identify the real from the fake. And while that may be true, I find that response a little heartless.

Artists shouldn't *have to* be in the NFT space just to prevent people from stealing their art and selling it as NFTs. Right now, NFTs are still the wild west, and they can, and will, benefit from more regulation and copyright protection. Still, for the time being, it's even more critical for an artist to be communicating with their audience about their involvement, or lack thereof, in the NFT space.

THE RICH GET RICHER

Doubling down on the "eat the rich" crusade, many people despise NFTs because rich people have gotten involved and gotten even richer (as if this doesn't happen in every industry anyway). While this is undoubtedly true, it doesn't mean that NFTs are inherently designed for rich people to come in and extract more wealth from the less wealthy. While I don't have numbers to cite, the NFT space can, and has, transformed many lives from lower middle class to obscene amounts of wealth, whether that's from getting lucky with a project they flipped or from launching a project of their own.

I know that's not particularly compelling, but keep in mind that most projects are launched for just a few hundred bucks in the inception, and some are even given away for free at launch. Even the Bored Ape Yacht Club was launched for around $300 worth of Ethereum, so there are certainly entry points for those without obscene wealth, but ultimately, it is a gamble to a degree.

Also playing a role in this idea that NFTs are for the rich is the ridiculous gas fees (transaction fees) associated with Ethereum-based NFTs. Another point I'll concede on because these gas fees are no joke. It can easily cost you upwards of $150 (USD) worth of ETH just in a transaction fee to buy an NFT. While that's certainly not always the case, it happens too often and can be a deterrent for many. For some context, I don't come from a lot of money or any money at all really, but I've been able to find success in the NFT space handling these fees, and I believe the contents of this book will do the same for you.

However, let's be more realistic and not rely on hope. Ethereum-based NFTs are just one ecosystem and one blockchain. Other blockchains like Solana or BNB have microscopic transaction fees compared to Ethereum's, often just cents or a few dollars. So right now, there are already alternative options that make it much more feasible for the little guy to get involved. Additionally, evolutions in Ethereum will be making gas fees more reasonable or even obsolete, as is the case with the NFT marketplace called Immutable X that allows the trading of Ethereum-based NFTs with ZERO gas fees.

NFTS ARE A SCAM

Many of the same people who claim Forex is a scam are yelling about how NFTs are a scam. In both instances, they are wrong. NFTs are *objectively* not scams, and there's no gray area to argue otherwise. Just like the Forex market and the internet, NFTs can absolutely be vehicles to carry out scams, and it happens often! That doesn't mean that NFTs as an industry or technology is a scam and when I hear people say that, it immediately discredits them in my eyes.

There are plenty of reputable projects and businesses in the NFT space. Some literally gave their NFTs out completely for free, didn't collect a dime at launch, and are still building and delivering value to their holders. Saying NFTs are a scam as a whole is 100% untrue and can easily be proven false just by pointing to the countless projects and businesses that aren't scams.

NFTS ARE A BUBBLE

For sure. The way NFTs are being used and overhyped right now is absolutely a bubble that will pop and allow the real projects and businesses to emerge. Much of what we see in the market as of 2021 and 2022 is irrationally priced and fueled by mania. I believe there will be a correction coming, especially for all of these lazy generative art projects. Until then, I'll continue to flip while also acquiring NFTs from projects positioning themselves as actual businesses that I believe will have longevity (we would call those types of projects Blue Chips).

So, in short, I would say NFTs *have* a bubble for many of their current uses but aren't necessarily a bubble as an industry as a whole.

UNNECESSARY DECENTRALIZATION

One of the proponents of the blockchain (and subsequently NFTs) is the decentralization of power and control, so a big corporation or government doesn't have it all. Many of the most zealous advocates for NFTs, crypto, and the blockchain despise centralization and want to decentralize everything under the sun. I'm a bit milder when it comes to decentralization, and I believe there's still plenty of room and need for centralization as well.

The blockchain's theoretically immutable and transparent nature is a dangerous thing for many people and in many industries. Although I'm sure there are secure and private solutions to be found somewhere, on a surface level, do we really want our medical records or car keys stored as NFTs on a public and distributed digital ledger? What if someone hacks our wallets and steals those assets? What if we lose access to our crypto wallet that stores these assets? The immutable and decentralized nature of the blockchain will make it incredibly difficult to recover those items and could put our privacy at tremendous risk.

Again, I believe there are smarter people than me who will have some reasonable solutions for those instances, and I see centralization as a key ingredient in many of those solutions. Decentralization is fantastic in many use cases, but it seems unnecessary to do it for everything blurb.

However, one instance where the decentralized nature of the blockchain is incredibly useful is during times of national distress or bank runs. For instance, during the war between Russia & Ukraine in 2022, some Ukrainian citizens had bank accounts frozen or inaccessible. Those who had assets on the blockchain had the ability to escape with all those assets secure and under their control.

Closing Remarks

You might have noticed in my responses to these objections that I agreed with most of them. I want to be honest that there are plenty of legitimate concerns surrounding the NFT space, but most people don't actually have a problem with NFTs. They have a problem with how they've seen them being used because, honestly, they're often used in pretty shitty ways. Other times, skeptics haven't fully wrapped their minds around what an NFT is and me saying that is a typical "crypto bro" thing to say because I'm basically saying, "oh, you just wouldn't understand." Nonetheless, it can sometimes be very accurate.

Regardless, the NFT world is messy, unregulated, and unrefined. It is these qualities that most have a gripe with, but I believe it comes with the territory of being an early adopter, and I know that the industry will necessarily improve and refine as it evolves and matures. I'm grateful to have people who challenge

NFTs since the space certainly needs a healthy skepticism considering the immense risk it carries. The truth is, there are brilliant people on both ends of the spectrum, and one of us will be dramatically wrong about the future of NFTs. I don't think it will be me.

3
WHY NFTS HAVE VALUE

We touched on the value of NFTs in the last two chapters, but now we're going to drive the point home. Many people ask, "why would someone even buy an NFT?"

The reality is, asking this is the same as asking, "Why would someone buy a product or service?" or "Why would someone invest in a business?" or "Why would someone buy an asset whose value may go up or down?"

There are as many answers to "why would anyone buy an NFT?" as there are products, services, assets, and businesses in the world. This is the case because any and everything can be integrated into the world of NFTs in one way or another. Right now, the NFT space is still the wild west, so there aren't always straightforward answers as to *how* a thing will be integrated, but there is certainly a way.

Now, we'll consider some of the most common reasons people are willing to spend money on NFTs.

Artwork

First is the art. Yes, believe it or not, some people still buy art purely because they like it. Whether digital or physical, there are still art collectors out there. Maybe they are hoping the value goes up in the future so they can flip it for a profit, or perhaps they just really liked it, and that's fine. I have personally bought physical and NFT art *just* because I liked it, without any intention of making money down the line. For some in the space, it's as simple as finding a piece they like, buying it, and holding on. And yes...you can display your NFT art physically as well. There are plenty of digital frames out there like TokenFrame that allows you to display your NFT art.

Support

Another related reason we see people spend their hard-earned money on NFTs is purely to be a supportive friend or fan. There are some NFTs inside my wallet that I may not even be crazy about, but I wanted to support my friend or an artist I've followed for years by buying one of their early NFTs. It's the same concept of spending money at a friend's business just to be supportive. Only in this case you more easily have the potential of reselling that asset you purchased if that particular friend or artist blows up in notoriety over the years.

Ownership Benefits & Utility

One of the main reasons I, and plenty of others, buy NFTs is for the utility and ownership benefits behind them. I'll provide some concrete details later in this chapter when we cover NFT use cases, but put simply, many NFTs go far beyond merely owning the visual piece that is the NFT. Owning certain NFTs may come with passive income, intellectual property rights, free assets, exclusive access or memberships, opportunities, voting rights, and a whole host of other ownership benefits. I often seek out long-term projects that offer a high level of professionalism and utility.

Flipping Potential

Other times, investors buy an NFT solely for the potential quick flip without considering the long-term value (if any). I also employ this approach myself, and I'll show you the ropes when we get to the NFT flipping strategies chapter towards the end of the book. Instead of looking at an NFT for its fundamentals, buying in for a flipping opportunity is usually done when there is a lot of hype and demand for the NFT project. Think of how many people will get in on a Yeezy release just to flip them on the secondary market. Same concept, but digital.

Community

Next up, we have the community. Some NFT projects have built up such an incredible community of founders and holders that people will spend money just to be a part of it. The idea of buying into a community angers many people who hate NFTs. Yet they seem just fine with concepts like country clubs, private organizations, golf clubs, rotary clubs, any type of club, really. There's a project called Sappy Seals that I bought intending to flip, but once a 3x flipping opportunity came, I decided to stay because the community was so immaculate, and I saw a bright future for them, hopefully with higher prices. Will I still flip? At some point, it's likely, but because the community is so strong, I'm willing to take the risk to get a 10x profit instead of just a 3x.

Metaverse

Now, let's talk about one of the most popular buzzwords right now: the "metaverse." The challenging part about all this metaverse talk is that nobody really knows what it means! Just about everyone you talk to about it will mean something different. And I've observed that most who speak about the metaverse haven't provided their audience the definition they're operating with. Because the metaverse is still a developing concept and therefore ill-defined, I'm not going to be calling anyone out and saying that their definition is bad, but I will provide one of my own that I believe is more all-encompassing of the various ingredients of this proposed metaverse. When most people use the term "metaverse," what they're referring to is a persistent, live, & immersive virtual world like what we see in the movie "Ready Player One." Matthew Ball has written an excellent perspective on this understanding of the metaverse that you can read here: https://www.matthewball.vc/all/themetaverse

My definition of the metaverse can be likened to that of the internet. And when you think about it like that, it makes sense why it can be hard to articulate. Think about how hard it would be to explain the internet to someone 100 years ago. If we tried to do that, we would never say that the internet is any one particular website, game, social media platform, app, or even internet service provider. Instead, Oxford Languages defines the internet as "a global computer network providing a variety of information and communication facilities, consisting of interconnected networks using standardized communication protocols." In other words, the internet is an interconnected web of a variety of technologies and platforms. Similarly, I would articulate the metaverse as being an interconnected web of a variety of technologies and platforms, including the blockchain, cryptocurrency, NFTs, virtual reality, augmented reality, virtual gaming, virtual worlds, and other related tech.

In fact, in Matthew Ball's article I just mentioned, you'll start to notice how all those elements I just mentioned play directly or indirectly into his outline of the metaverse. As of now, there is not one single "metaverse." Many people ask me, "Jared, how do I enter the metaverse?" And my answer is always, "it depends on what you mean by metaverse." Typically they're asking how to interact with these immersive virtual worlds that are often considered microcosms of the metaverse like Cryptovoxels, Decentraland, Somnium Space, etc.

So, for now, most businesses, teams, and individuals are working more on their own idea or version of the metaverse, and they'll all look a bit different with varying levels of centralization, but what we're seeing a push towards is ownership inside the metaverse being determined by NFTs. This brings me to the next reason someone would buy an NFT: ownership inside the metaverse.

Let's think back to that movie, Ready Player One. First, you'll need to go and watch that movie after this book as a refresher, but if you haven't already, then at least go watch a 3-minute trailer of it to get some context. In short, the movie tells the story of a dystopian future for Earth where people's only escape from a crude reality was going inside of this persistent, always live, immersive world entered via a virtual reality headset and an optional full-body haptic suit (to feel sensations inside the virtual world). Inside this virtual world, players can have ownership over assets like cars, clothes, skins, weapons, and real estate. I believe, as we already see, that when this type of virtual environment, or metaverse, becomes our reality, ownership of those assets will be in the form of NFTs.

For example, you've likely already seen the headlines of multi-million dollar plots of virtual land being sold.

While most virtual land is much cheaper than that, people who own these virtual plots are considered to own land in the metaverse (even if it's just a microcosm of the metaverse). So all these mini metaverses we have like Cryptovoxels, Decentraland, and Somnium Space all have their own separate ecosystems and land markets where people can buy plots of land to build on.

Now, you may be wondering why anyone would spend real money on fake land? The reality is that the same ways people can monetize physical land can also apply to digital land. We'll dive into the specifics later in this chapter when we get to the virtual real estate section.

Status Symbols

One of the last reasons people buy NFTs that I'll mention, although there are plenty more, is for the status or clout. Yes, it's true; some NFTs are purchased because of the status that comes with owning them. This is not a reason to hate them, however. Just like you and I can go to a Walmart or Target and pick up a $20 wristwatch that will tell the same time as a $100,000 Rolex, there are still people who will go and buy that Rolex and a wide variety of status symbols just because they can afford it, or it's their taste.

THE NFT EQUATION   57

The same can be said of some NFTs. The famous Cryptopunks were at one point given away for free in their early days, and they are now going for millions despite having little to no actual utility. Some purchasers of the Cryptopunks will certainly have purchased because they are a historical piece of NFT history, but many others did indeed buy for the status & clout.

Remember, none of these reasons for buying an NFT are mutually exclusive, and there will frequently be a combination of them that ultimately lead to a purchase.

Looking beyond the reasons we just considered, the value of NFTs also falls right back to the blockchain tech they are built on top of. Like the blockchain, NFTs function as proof of authenticity, proof of ownership, and immutability. Still, right now, you may see all of this as a "theoretical" value, but let's take a look at how this proposed value is actively being applied by examining some of today's most common use cases for NFTs.

AVATAR/CHARACTER STYLE & PROFILE PICTURES (PFP)

The use case most people are used to seeing is the avatar-style, character-based generative projects that are often used as profile pictures to help with brand awareness and community building.

Think of projects like the Cryptopunks & Bored Ape Yacht Club. Those would fall under this category because they have a base character and each NFT in the collection has a different set of traits that make them unique and more or less rare than others.

This style of project is the one most commonly under attack by NFT critics because the focus is on the artwork without consideration of ownership benefits & utility. While it is true that most projects of this style don't have utility, many others do. The Enigma Economy project we saw earlier in this book, for example, would fall under this type of project but has an incredibly unique utility since each NFT is connected to a particular hash rate in a crypto mining facility.

A common utility for these projects is shared intellectual property (IP) rights. Many of these projects will grant IP rights of the character or avatar to the holder of the NFT. For instance, the Bored Ape Yacht Club offers this exact setup as one of their utilities. In the typical digital world, it would be a violation of copyright laws to simply take an image of someone else's creative work and monetize it for your own benefit. However, as long as you own a Bored Ape, you have some IP rights over that particular ape that allows you to monetize it in ways that you see fit.

One holder even created a wine brand using his Bored Apes as the mascots & branding for the company. Whether that wine brand continued or had any success, I'm not sure, but you can imagine the power of having IP rights over a character or family of characters that have a global presence. The Bored Ape Yacht Club could even go on to create an animated TV series where holders could get paid to have their apes appear in the series as characters. It's only a matter of time before an NFT project does precisely this and has massive success with their series and ends up putting their holders in a position to make even more money!

As you dive deeper into the space, you'll start to notice how these avatar-style projects can quite easily be entwined with a variety of other use cases we'll look at and how they're almost always more than a pretty picture.

ARTS & MEDIA

Of course, we have the arts and media sector getting into the world of NFTs. This is where the common misconception comes from that NFTs are just digital art pieces. Whether an artist creates physical art, digital art, sculptures, poems, spoken word, music, or any other art form, they can integrate their work into the NFT space in a way that works for them.

While some of these NFTs will have added utility beyond the art, some are solely focused on the art, and that's fine. Like physical art, many buy these to support artists & friends or for their personal enjoyment and pride of ownership.

An example of an art or media-based NFT with utility would be what hip hop artist Nas recently did with his NFT project. He launched a series of NFTs on the Royal platform, allowing whoever owns the NFT to receive a small percentage of his streaming royalties. This is an incredible example of how artists can put themselves *and* their communities on by literally paying the people who support you by purchasing NFTs and streaming your music.

DIGITAL COLLECTIBLES

Have you ever heard of trading cards? Whether it's sports cards or gaming-related cards like Pokemon, you likely understand the concept of trading cards and how crazy passionate people can get in that realm. And, of course, trading cards are just the tip of the iceberg when it comes to physical collectibles. People will pay a pretty penny for collectibles of just about any kind: cars, clothes, signatures, footballs, coins, buttons, pins, rocks, vinyl records, and tons of others.

Similarly, people want digital collectibles as well. Sometimes it'll be for potential resale value, and other times simply for the pride of ownership. The NBA Top Shot NFT platform was created to capitalize on people's love for basketball and their desire to own a moment in history. The platform highlights clips of past and current moments from NBA games and turns them into collectible clips in the form of NFTs.

Last I checked, the NFL is working on a similar project as well.

GAMING

Pay **very** close attention to the world of gaming as it integrates with NFTs. I believe that the gaming industry will bring NFTs and crypto to mass adoption. In theory, NFTs offer greater monetization opportunities for gamers as they can now truly own in-game assets. In traditional gaming, when a player wants to buy an in-game asset like a skin or weapon upgrade, they go to the developer (in-game), buy that asset, it goes into their account to be used, and that's the end of the story. With NFTs integrated, that in-game asset would be an NFT that goes into the player's crypto wallet connected to their account. Once the player no longer wants the in-game asset they paid for, they can simply list it for sale and allow another player to purchase it from them (potentially for a profit). NFTs being integrated into gaming also offers the potential for players themselves to more easily contribute in-game assets as NFTs that can be bought and sold amongst each other.

From another angle, we also have NFTs that function as your in-game character or avatar and enable a play-to-earn (P2E) model to be easily integrated into the gaming ecosystem. This P2E gaming model essentially allows those who own an NFT character of the game to play the game and earn some of that game's native cryptocurrency coin that can be used to buy in-game assets or converted to other crypto or fiat. This sounds great, but if that game's currency isn't worth anything, they are playing to earn a worthless cryptocurrency coin. However, if that game has immense success and a thriving community, that coin's value could easily increase and potentially be paying players thousands of dollars worth of their native crypto.

Axie Infinity would be a project to study in the P2E model. In order to play this game, you need to own an NFT of one of the characters inside the game, and once you begin playing, you have the opportunity to earn their native currency if you win against other players.

Coming at gaming from a different angle is the NFT 2040 project. This first-person shooter gaming project launched a genesis NFT collection of weapon crates that function as the holder's early access ticket to a beta version of a video game designed around NFT avatar-style projects. Their goal is to integrate a variety of avatar-style projects that can be played as characters inside the game. For instance, a 3D model version of a bored ape has already been created and is visible in early demo gameplay footage of the game.

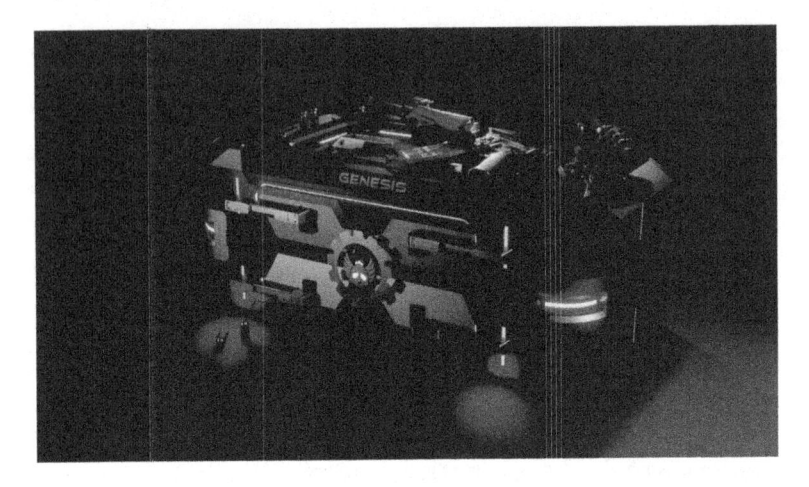

This powerful concept plays into the cult-like following many NFT projects have already garnered. In this game, you can import your 2D NFT avatar into a 3D virtual gaming environment where you can compete against other NFT projects that look entirely different than yours. To top it all off, they are planning to have a P2E feature in the game in the future.

Circling back to that genesis NFT for NFT 2040, those who hold that NFT will receive a variety of free airdropped NFT assets that are compatible in-game (in-game assets) and will be denoted as early supporters in-game along with a handful of other ownership benefits.

We've only scratched the surface of the power NFTs will have in the gaming industry, but, unfortunately, there are a plethora of gaming veterans and industry experts who vehemently despise NFTs and their integration into traditional gaming. Many of their objections stem from various misconceptions about NFTs, but time will be the ultimate judge of NFTs' viability in gaming.

VIRTUAL LAND

We already discussed the concept of virtual plots of land inside these various "metaverses," but allow me to provide a very clear reason that this land is even valuable in the first place. As I mentioned, these virtual plots of land (which are NFTs) can be monetized in many of the same ways physical land can be.

One of the most common ways to monetize virtual land is to build an art exhibit or museum. Once someone has acquired a bare plot of land, they can start building on it, and an art-focused building is common since, in many of these virtual worlds, you can embed NFTs directly on the walls of your building. Landowners may showcase their own NFT art inside or even offer paid promotions where they have other artists pay them just to get a spot inside their metaverse art show.

Similarly, landowners can sell ad space to businesses or individuals. Of course, your location and ability to drive traffic to your plot of land will be a big factor in whether or not anyone is willing to pay to advertise on your land, but it's certainly a possibility.

Did you know that there have already been several business conferences and music concerts inside these virtual worlds (especially Decentraland)? That's right! So what if you created an event venue on the land you own and rented it out to people looking to hold events inside the metaverse? Boom, another opportunity to monetize.

And you can, of course, simply buy land with the intention to flip it! Just like physical land, you can buy it, do zero development or building, and just may be able to flip it for a profit.

On the other side of this virtual land are the designers who create the buildings and structures in 3D modeling programs. There are already metaverse architecture firms that get paid to do this regularly. So if you have a skill set in the area of 3D modeling, you have an opportunity to be contracted to develop on land that someone else owns, just like in the real world, but without all the risk and overhead.

If you were deeply confused about why anyone would spend a dime on this virtual land, hopefully now you recognize a few rational reasons as to why they do. When we start considering the parallels this NFT virtual land has to physical land, it helps us wrap our minds around why people are spending thousands or millions of dollars on it.

MEMBERSHIPS, ACCESS, TICKETS

This use case is commonly integrated with many other use cases (like avatars) to add an extra layer of utility. Thanks to the ability to easily prove authenticity and ownership over NFTs, many events and clubs can use them as membership cards or tickets to events. Coachella has recently unveiled its plans to offer a handful of NFTs that provide lifetime access to Coachella's events! I'm confident we will see more and more of this for music events.

Sometimes there are clubs or VIP sections of clubs that are only accessible by certain NFTs (Bored Apes have done this). Other times you'll find certain websites or discords that are "token-gated" where only those who connect their wallets and verify ownership of a particular NFT will be able to access it.

Gary Vaynerchuck has a token-gated website for his VeeFriends NFT holders that allows them to log in with their wallets and access or claim certain benefits unique to them. Simultaneously, his VeeFriends NFTs also function as tickets to his annual VeeCon business conference.

ALTERNATIVE PAYMENT METHODS

Some NFTs will simply be an alternative way to pay for a product or service, and that's it. Meaning instead of someone paying in fiat money (like USD) for a product or service, they will pay cryptocurrency by purchasing an NFT.

For example, I have sold an ebook where people could go on my sales page and choose whether they want to pay in fiat or crypto. If they want to pay in crypto, they'll click a link that takes them to the NFT marketplace called Rarible, where they'll see a 3D photo of the ebook. That 3D image is technically what they are buying when they purchase the NFT. So, now the question is, how do they get the actual PDF ebook? The answer is in the "unlockable content."

Unlockable content within an NFT is typically just a text box that can only be accessed by those who have the NFT inside their wallet. So, in this case, once someone has purchased my ebook NFT, they'll be able to open the unlockable content where they will find a link directly to the PDF file where they can read or download it.

Although I did add a little cherry on top for the NFT edition by offering lifetime updates to it for free to NFT holders, overall, there is very little difference between buying the NFT edition with crypto vs buying the traditional way using fiat money. So in this instance, the NFT's use case was primarily to facilitate an alternative payment method. Sometimes it can be as simple as that.

DECENTRALIZED AUTONOMOUS ORGANIZATIONS (DAOS)

There are nearly limitless amounts of use cases for NFTs because of their ability to integrate into anything, but, in an effort not to overwhelm or confuse, the last use case we'll look at in this chapter is a decentralized autonomous organization or DAO.

Traditional business structures are hierarchical. Meaning there is a person, or people, at the top of the organization making big decisions for the company without much reliance on the decision-making ability of everyone else inside the organization. Visually, this structure looks like a pyramid.

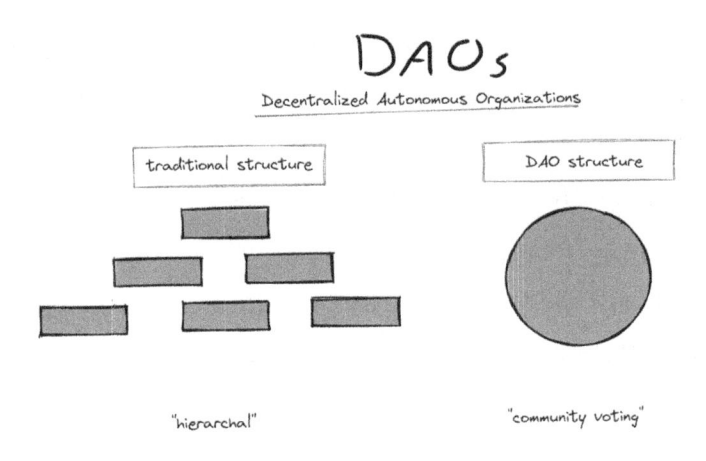

DAOs
Decentralized Autonomous Organizations

| traditional structure | DAO structure |

"hierarchal"   "community voting"

On the other hand, a DAO business structure is more like a circle where decision-making is at least partially decentralized and distributed amongst the members of the organization. Depending on the varying degree of decentralization a DAO has implemented, there will typically still be a team of founders that will lead and drive the project. Still, many of their decisions for the company will depend on what their community votes on.

Put simply, in a DAO business structure, the community of token holders (in this case NFTs) are the ones who make the company decisions instead of a president or CEO. Then, the founding team will be responsible for executing the final decision. In application, this voting will typically take place on a web 3 platform like Snapshot.org that allows DAOs to set up their voting mechanism and enable token holders to connect their wallets, verify ownership, and then cast their votes on decisions for the company's next move.

How decisions are made

Community Generates Conversations & Ideas

↓

Options are compiled

↓

Votes are cast by token holders

↓

execution

Recalling the Enigma Economy project, they've already used that platform multiple times to make community decisions such as our reinvestment schedule and what currencies we will be mining during certain periods.

DAOs are becoming an increasingly attractive business structure. However, there's still plenty of room to refine and improve how this model is executed and the extent of decentralization for each project. Most types of group decision-making can be structured into DAOs if it makes sense for the kind of decisions that the group will be making.

Well then, we've covered a handful of NFT use cases in this chapter that have ideally painted a very clear picture of why some NFTs may be valuable. Again, not all NFTs will fall into one of these use case categories, and plenty will fall into multiple. None are necessarily better than another because it totally depends on the structure and founders of the project that will add more value and longevity, not the use case.

Now that you've garnered a good base of understanding and context, we're going to move into some action-taking steps and clearly articulate how you can begin interacting with the world of NFTs.

Are NFTs making more sense to you yet? If so, I'd really appreciate you taking a few minutes to write a quick review for this book on Amazon, sharing how it's helped you gain a better understanding!

You can visit nftequation.com/bookreview to post your review.

4
THE EXACT STEPS TO GET STARTED INVESTING OR CREATING

Necessary Tools & Resources

Meta Mask
Metamask is one of many wallets that easily integrates into your Google Chrome or Brave Browser to allow you to interact with Web 3.0 & buy/sell NFTs.

Laptop or Desktop
The preferred medium of interacting with NFT marketplaces & Web 3.0

Ethereum
You'll need some ETH to cover gas fees & pay for the NFTs that you would like to collect.

Cell Phone
Smartphones can be an alternative, but are more prone to bugs and errors.

This chapter will walk you step by step through the process of getting the necessary accounts and assets in place to begin your NFT journey. This is a chapter you may want to bookmark for future reference as I've found that there aren't too many places to find these steps as clearly explained as you'll find here. Without further ado, let's dive in.

PRELIMINARY STEPS

Tech Requirements - Don't panic. There is no special tech required to get involved in the NFT space! The good news is all you need is a laptop, really. While you can do just about everything we'll cover in this book on most smartphones, you'll be far more prone to encounter costly errors, delays, and bugs than doing it on your laptop. So if a phone is all you've got, don't give up, but try your best to invest in a cheap laptop.

Once you get that laptop, make sure you've got Google Chrome or Brave Browser installed, and then you can go to their respective app stores and download the Metamask extension, which we'll talk about a bit later. Once you've done that, you've satisfied the basic tech requirements to get into it.

Social Media - Being on the right social media platforms is vital to your success and agility in the NFT space. The reality is NFTs live and breathe on Twitter and Discord so having accounts for both is non-negotiable. It doesn't matter what your opinion or experience is with them...you need accounts for these. Twitter is used for staying updated on the latest news in the NFT world & following your favorite influencers and leaders in the space. Remember, the NFT space moves at the speed of light, and Twitter does too. As for Discord, just about every project will host their community within their Discord server to stay in touch, deliver ownership benefits, provide updates, and talk amongst each other.

Now that we've got those taken care of let's get into the real action items.

STEP 1 - SETTING UP YOUR WALLET

First and foremost, we need to get you your first (or the correct) cryptocurrency wallet. Crypto wallets are used to store blockchain-based assets like cryptocurrencies and NFTs, so don't think they're *just* for crypto. There is no shortage of wallets out there, and they'll serve different purposes and work with different blockchains. If you're new to the blockchain as a whole, you'll soon start to realize that you need maybe a dozen different wallets to be fully equipped, but let's not overwhelm you with that thought just yet.

For now, all you need to do is head over to both your mobile app store and Google Chrome Web Store and download the Metamask extension. The best way to get to the right place is to go to the official Metamask website at https://metamask.io/ and use the links provided there.

Metamask is simply a cryptocurrency wallet that allows you to store blockchain-based assets like crypto & NFTs and connect to Web 3.0 platforms and dApps. While Metamask is optimized for assets based on the Ethereum blockchain, you can also configure it to work with some others. However, don't worry yourself about that right now, and just know that you'll be using Metamask exclusively for Ethereum-based assets, as it's the topic of our conversation in this book.

As you begin learning and growing in this world, you'll start hearing about other people using different wallets than Metamask for the same stuff you're doing. People often use wallets like Coinbase & Trust Wallet to interact with the world of NFTs. While those wallets can certainly work, it's been proven time and time again that they are *far* more prone to encountering errors and bugs with NFT platforms. Right now, Metamask is the industry standard for wallets that will be tested and optimized for on NFT marketplaces and project websites. So, unless you're already skilled in the

NFT space, don't try to be fancy by using a wallet of your choice; get Metamask.

Once you have your Metamask app and extension downloaded, we've got to set it up and sync your accounts. Let's start with the browser extension on your laptop.

A new tab should open after it's successfully installed that welcomes you to Metamask with a "Get Started" button right below. Upon pressing that button, you'll be taken to a screen that asks if you'd like to set up a new wallet or import a wallet. The import option is for syncing an already existing wallet to this new device (like what we'll do to sync your mobile and laptop Metamask accounts), but since this is likely your first time, just choose the new wallet option.

You'll then be asked to create a password, so create something secure that you don't use for anything else. And I know you're always told to use a password that you don't use for anything else, but you do anyway. This needs to be the exception. This is not something to play with or be lazy about. Create a brand new, complex password that can't be easily guessed and isn't recorded digitally.

After that, you'll come to a page that gives you a brief overview of what a "secret recovery phrase" is. Also called a seed phrase or secret phrase, your secret recovery phrase is a series of random words (in this case 12) that will be able to bypass the password you just set up. Anyone with access to this seed phrase will have full access to everything inside your wallet. Be sure you watch the short video explainer they provide on that page for a little more context.

Following that, you'll receive your very own secret recovery phrase (seed phrase) that you'll be responsible for securing and storing appropriately. Under no circumstance should you store this digitally or share this with anyone. Do not take a screenshot or picture of this seed phrase. Do not write this seed phrase down in your notes and rename the file and think it's safe. I wouldn't even store this in a password manager personally. The *best* way to secure this seed phrase is to write it down with pen and paper or even order a specialized piece of metal designed for storing seed phrases where you carve it in. Assuming you only have the paper, that'll do for now. Write it down about three times and split it up into different safe places (bank deposit vault, your home safe, etc.).

Ideally, you'd memorize the phrase and have no written trace of it all, but that's likely not practical for most people. There are a variety of additional security measures that you can take, like splitting up the seed phrase words into segments and hiding them in different states or countries. This might seem dramatic, but remember, this is the wild west right now, and if you get scammed out of your assets, there's no bank or organization to adequately compensate you for your losses. You get scammed... you're shit out of luck.

Just know, storing your phrase in any digital capacity is a great way to maximize your risk to a whole host of vulnerabilities; do not do it. Also, there will **never** come a time when anyone should ask for your seed phrase. Not even the Metamask support team will ask for that, and there are always impersonators posing as Metamask support and asking for seed phrases. If someone asks for your seed phrase, they are trying to scam you.

Now that we've covered that bit and you've recorded your seed phrase, you'll come to the final screen that says congratulations. So we've set up Metamask on a laptop/desktop, but how do we sync this wallet to your mobile device?

It's pretty easy. Open up the mobile app and select the import wallet option. It should then ask you to either import your seed phrase or your private keys. Private keys are another password circumventing access method to your wallet, and they're called "private" for a reason. Your private keys should also never be shared with anyone.

If it asks for your seed phrase, go ahead and enter that, and your wallets will be synced up so they're the same on mobile and laptop. If they ask for your private keys, click on the Metamask extension in your browser, hit the three vertical dots to the right of the wallet name (right under your profile picture), select "account details," choose "export private key," and enter your Metamask password. You'll now be able to view your private keys that you can type into your mobile app.

Once you've done that correctly, you'll successfully have set up your Metamask wallet, good job!

Hardware vs Digital Wallets

You just set up what we would call a digital, or "hot," wallet because your wallet's information is stored entirely online and always connected to the internet. Even without your seed phrase recorded digitally, this hot wallet is still more vulnerable than the alternative: cold wallets.

A cold wallet, also called a hardware wallet, is a type of cryptocurrency wallet that allows you to store your assets and security information on a physical device that is **not** connected to the internet. Instead, it is plugged into your computer when you're ready to buy, sell, or move blockchain assets like crypto and NFTs. This means cold wallets are much more secure than your typical online-only wallet like what we just set up.

Hot wallets are still great to use (I use plenty), but a hardware wallet is just that extra layer of security and an absolute **must-have** if you're serious about this space. I recommend you pick up a Ledger Nano X, which I have myself. You can buy one from the official Ledger site using my affiliate link jaredtross.com/ledger.

That link will take you directly to the official ledger website, and that is the ONLY place you should ever buy a Ledger wallet. Don't ever buy them from third parties like friends, family, eBay, Amazon, Walmart, or anywhere other than the manufacturer's website itself. If you do, you run the risk of the wallet being tampered with before getting to you, thus compromising its security. Do not try to go bargain hunting and find it cheaper elsewhere; pay the price Ledger is selling it for and sleep better at night.

Consider this; if you connect your hot Metamask wallet to a malicious website, the attackers could potentially access the assets inside your wallet and approve transactions remotely because it's always connected to the internet. If you connect your Ledger hardware wallet to a malicious site, it's still very dangerous, but your assets can't be stolen without you physically pressing buttons to confirm & allow it on your Ledger device. I store assets in both hot and cold wallets, but my most valuable assets will always be moved over to my Ledger wallet.

Ledgers will also come with a seed phrase that you should treat in the same way as you would treat a hot wallet seed phrase, so be sure to keep that safe as well. Keep in mind that there are a variety of hardware wallets out there, and Ledger is just one brand, but there are others that are also totally legit, but again Ledger has been the standard in the circles I'm involved in.

The good news is, you can easily integrate your Ledger with your Metamask (while still keeping your assets offline and secure, of course), but that's a step for a later date because even if you ordered your Ledger right now, you'd have some time to wait before it gets to you.

STEP 2 - ACQUIRING CRYPTOCURRENCY

Now that you've created your wallet, it's time to fund it. After all, these NFTs will cost you some money (unless you get into a project that is giving their NFTs away for free at launch, yes they exist).

There are various ways that you can acquire some cryptocurrency, but I'm just going to cover the primary methods I use to do it, which are pretty straightforward. Keep in mind there are thousands of different cryptocurrencies out there, but our goal here is to convert some of our fiat money (USD, for example) into Ethereum (ETH)

First, you can simply purchase ETH directly inside Metamask using their payment processing partners, Wyre or Transak. To do this, just click on your Metamask extension and hit the big "BUY" button where you'll be able to choose your payment option. If you're unsure which to pick, just roll the dice or click on Wyre since it doesn't make that big of a difference in my experience.

Once on the payment screen, go ahead and insert the appropriate payment details using your debit card and proceed to processing the payment. If you're wondering how much to buy, only risk what you can afford to lose, but a good, arbitrary starting point is $1,000-$2,500 (USD) worth of ETH. Again, you risk what you can afford to lose, but buy at least $500 (USD) worth of ETH to get yourself started.

Now, you may have encountered a payment processing error. Sometimes, the answer could be as simple as trying again and confirming you input all the correct info (especially your zip code). You may also need to verify your identity according to the platform's requirements, so do that if Wyre or Transak requests it. Other times, your bank may be the culprit. In some cases, you may need to call your bank's fraud department and tell them to allow the transaction. If you do this, make sure to stay on the line with them until the transaction goes through to make sure they listen to you.

Still encountering issues? If you live in Texas or NY (meaning your billing address for your card is in those places, or you verified your identity with a license in those places), you're likely restricted on Wyre & Transak from buying cryptocurrency. Don't worry; there's a solution for you. Also, if you bank with Chase, as of February 2022, they informed me they are no longer allowing cryptocurrency purchases. Again, don't worry if any of those situations apply to you and you're unable to buy ETH directly from Metamask.

One of the big reasons banks are tightening their grip on allowing customers to buy cryptocurrency is that crypto transactions can be more challenging to track. They'll tell you it's for their customer's safety (which I'm sure is partially true), but ultimately they and the government want to know what we're up to. More decentralized platforms like Metamask don't necessarily play well with that objective.

So the first alternative you have is using a more centralized platform like Coinbase. As you spend more time in the crypto and NFT space, you'll come across many crypto veterans who despise centralized platforms like Coinbase because they have more control and influence over your assets that, in theory, are supposed to be entirely in your control in the blockchain world. These people are certainly right, but I still encourage new people to get their start on centralized, easy-to-use platforms like Coinbase because it's a great starting point! Not a place to keep your assets long-term, that's for sure, but Coinbase is a fantastic option to get your foot in the door and start learning the ropes. Coinbase is the most popular centralized exchange and wallet for blockchain assets. If you're having difficulty purchasing your ETH via Metamask's partners, you'll likely have more success by creating a Coinbase account and verifying your identity.

Once you've set up your account and linked your bank and debit cards, you should be able to complete a purchase without any major hiccups. Coinbase will typically put a variety of limitations on new accounts. So, if you just got set up and verified, do not be alarmed to find a limit on your max purchase and a time limit before you can transfer or use the crypto you just purchased. An annoying aspect, but those limits should be reduced or removed as your account ages a few weeks or months.

After successfully acquiring some ETH inside of your Coinbase account, you'll then need to send it over to your Metamask wallet. This is a straightforward process, but I'll walk you through it in case this is your first time sending crypto. Just about every crypto wallet will have a wallet address that uniquely identifies it. These public addresses will typically be a series of randomly generated numbers and letters. For example, one of my wallet addresses is: 0x8B9003895229E4025Ee62F977d3ac11C7D7fA799

This wallet address is PUBLIC, so it's not a security risk for people to see this. After all, they'll need it to be able to send you crypto and NFTs in the future, and anytime you buy or sell an NFT, everyone will be able to see your address. Recall that the blockchain is a public digital ledger of transactions that anyone can see. This means that if someone has your wallet address, they can see every transaction you've ever made on the blockchain and everything inside your wallet, and that's okay! That's the nature of the blockchain, but there are certainly ways to make sure some wallet addresses have little to no public trace back to you if you're really concerned.

Anyways, you can find your Metamask wallet address by clicking on your Metamask extension icon, and right below your wallet's name, you'll find an abbreviated version of your address that should start with "0x......." All you need to do is click on it, and the address will be copied to your clipboard.

Ethereum Mainnet

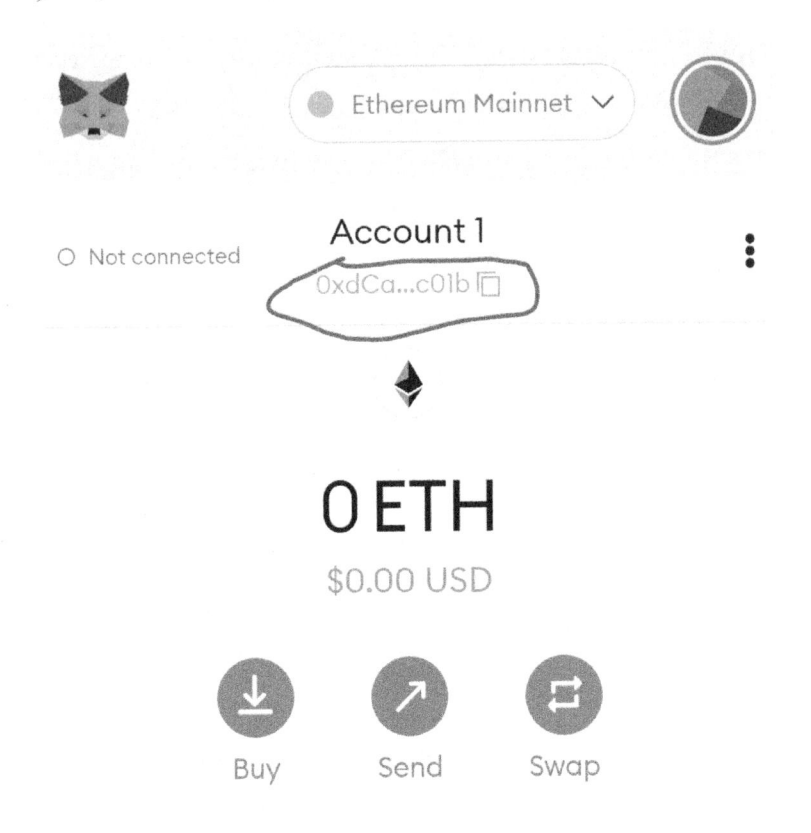

Not connected

Account 1
0xdCa...c01b

0 ETH
$0.00 USD

Buy   Send   Swap

Now, head back to Coinbase and click on your ETH balance/wallet. Once there, you should see some options on the right-hand side to send and receive ETH. If you wanted to send ETH to your Coinbase or have someone else send you some, you'd select the receive option where you'd find both a QR code and your wallet address that you could share either of with the sender in order to receive some crypto. In our case, we want to send ETH from this Coinbase account to another wallet, so click send and paste in the Metamask address we just copied.

Proceed through the steps and enter however much you want to send over to your Metamask. If you're new to all this, I highly recommend you send a tiny fraction (maybe $20 worth of ETH) of your total amount as a test transaction just to confirm you didn't miss anything or copy and paste the wrong thing. A few minutes after your test transaction is sent, you should be able to see your balance updated inside Metamask. With that confirmation, go ahead and repeat the process to send the rest of your funds.

While Coinbase is particularly useful if you're a US Citizen, the next route I outline will be an option for those that can't, or won't, use Coinbase.

Paxful is a peer-to-peer, global trading platform that is useful for people who may not be able to, or want to, acquire their crypto through a typical exchange platform like Coinbase. If you have trouble accessing certain platforms because of your location or citizenship, Paxful can be a great alternative. Using this platform, you can find individuals who are willing to sell their crypto, at a premium, for a variety of over 350 payment methods, including gift cards and prepaid cards.

Depending on where you live, you may need to download and set up a VPN to access the platform, as they prohibit a few regions. A VPN can change your apparent location so you can interact with it and acquire some crypto.

If you still can't find a way to get yourself some ETH, you may need to reach out to friends or family who can, and they can then send you the crypto directly. You can also just do a Google search on acquiring crypto in your location or situation. No matter the route you have to take, get some ETH and put it inside a Metamask wallet.

If you'd like to claim your free video training and see a video tutorial of setting up your Metamask and acquiring ETH, please visit https://www.nftequation.com/bookbonus or text BONUS to 214-466-1640 (my direct line) for your free NFT Masterclass.

STEP 3 - CONNECTING TO AN NFT MARKETPLACE

The final step to get yourself set up to begin buying and selling NFTs is to connect your wallet to an NFT marketplace. NFT marketplaces are very similar to traditional marketplaces you're already used to, like Facebook Marketplace, eBay, Craigslist, etc. On these NFT marketplaces, people can list NFTs for sale, buy them, make offers, and even create their own.

Although there are dozens of marketplaces, this book will primarily focus on two of the most popular; Opensea & Rarible. Much of what we'll discuss will also apply to the many other marketplaces.

NFT Marketplaces

Opensea
Opensea, like Rarible, is a very user-friendly NFT marketplace to buy and sell NFTs.

Rarible
Rarible is a mostly art-focused NFT Marketplace that you can easily mint and sell your NFTs on.

LooksRare
LooksRare is a fairly new NFT marketplace intended to rival Opensea and address many of its shortcomings.

Foundation
Foundation is a platform that aims to build a new creative economy with an emphasis on arts.

Sol Sea
An NFT marketplace similar to Opensea, but designed for NFTs based on the Solana (SOL) blockchain.

Unlike a platform like eBay, where you click sign up and enter your email and password to create an account, many NFT marketplaces will have you sign in or sign up by connecting your Metamask wallet. In these instances, your wallet address will function as your username unless you manually add a username for your new account.

First, let's head over to Opensea by typing into your browser: opensea.io and hitting enter. On the top of your screen, all the way to the right, you'll see an icon that resembles a wallet. Click on that, and you'll be met with a few options that will allow you to connect a variety of wallets. Keep it simple and select the Metamask option. At that point, your Metamask wallet should open up and ask you to confirm that you want to connect to the platform. Hit confirm, and your wallet has now been connected to Opensea, and you have an account set up; good job! Feel free to go in and add a profile picture, username, link your socials, and all that other good stuff, but there's no need to at the moment.

Next, we can do the same thing over on Rarible. Rarible's URL is just: www.rarible.com

Once there, you'll see a sign-in button that, once clicked, will take you to a page with a few different wallet options. Again, click on Metamask, wait for the request to pop up, and confirm it. Simple as that, you've now set up a profile on Rarible as well!

Both Opensea & Rarible are non-custodial, meaning your NFTs aren't actively stored on their platform (they don't have custody). This is a big point of confusion for many beginners because what you'll notice is that once you have bought some NFTs, they'll be visible both on your Rarible profile and your Opensea profile. While not all marketplaces are non-custodial, think of platforms such as Rarible and Opensea as more like display cases for your NFTs. The reason they show up on different marketplaces is because you have the same wallet connected to both platforms, and the actual NFTs are stored inside your Metamask wallet.

I hope I've detailed this process clearly enough for you to get everything situated without any issues. As a reminder, I do have a free NFT masterclass that walks you through this process visually at https://www.nftequation.com/bookbonus.

In this next chapter, I'll walk you through the process of actually buying your very first NFT!

5
HOW TO BUY YOUR FIRST NFT

This is a very exciting chapter for you, as by the end, you should have purchased your first NFT. This is also a very dangerous chapter because, by the end, you should have purchased your first NFT.

It's both exciting and dangerous because once you buy your first, it's very hard to stop buying more! I've found it's a rare occurrence to find someone who has purchased an NFT but hasn't bought many more within a few weeks. Anyway, let's focus up and get into the step-by-step breakdown on how to do it.

STEP 1 - WALLET & OPENSEA SET UP

Well, look at that; you're already done with step 1, which was to get your Metamask and Opensea account set up. Optionally, you can do this process on another NFT marketplace like Rarible, but I'll focus on Opensea here.

STEP 2 - DETERMINE YOUR OBJECTIVE & SELECT AN NFT

You ought to have some type of reason for your purchase instead of just buying an NFT because it's an NFT. Your buying objective can certainly change from purchase to purchase but go in with some intention.

Some possible buying objectives may be:

- Quick flip - Buying an NFT without caring much about the fundamentals. Only interested in capitalizing off of hype for a quick flip.
- Utility - Buying an NFT to take advantage of the ownership benefits or utilities.
- Supporting Others - Buying an NFT just because you want to support an artist you love or a friend you care about.

- Storing Value - Buying an NFT because it has a strong team and strong fundamentals (we'll talk about this in a few chapters) that you believe will continue to grow in value over the years.
- Just for fun - Buying an NFT just because you like it.

Of course, there are plenty of other reasons for buying NFTs, but we'll keep it simple just to give you some options to consider. However, I will almost always recommend that for your VERY FIRST NFT, you buy one purely because you like it and it's cheap. I highly discourage beginners from buying their first NFT with the intention of making a profit.

Instead, browse Opensea or Rarible and find an NFT that's super cheap that you personally like the look of. Rarity doesn't matter. Utility doesn't matter. Flipping potential doesn't matter. Just buy something super cheap that you'd be happy to hold even if it was worthless. I did exactly this when I first started. The reason I recommend this is because I want you to first be familiar with the process so that you're not caught by surprise as you begin actively investing.

If your main goal is to create and sell NFTs, then this step of buying one first is just as important! Many people interested in the creator side of NFTs are so eager to make and sell some that they don't even bother buying one. Why is this problematic? Because they just created something with a very limited perspective and have no first-hand experience going through the customer journey. How much sense would it make for someone to open up a car dealership without ever going through the car buying process? They're likely to miss many steps or, at the very least, be unhelpful when a potential customer has questions or concerns about the process. You want to be intimately familiar with the variety of ways to purchase an NFT before you start trying to sell them.

With that said, you should now have determined your purchasing objective and identified an NFT that you're ready to purchase. Make sure in your browsing process that you've found an NFT that is on the Ethereum blockchain (will have a black ETH logo next to the price) and not ETH on polygon, which will have a purple ETH logo. Polygon is fine, but not what we want for right now.

THE NFT EQUATION   101

STEP 3 - CLICK THE BUY NOW BUTTON

Assuming that you've already funded your Metamask wallet and are logged in to Opensea on the listing page of the NFT you want to buy, the next step is pretty straightforward...click on the "buy now" button.

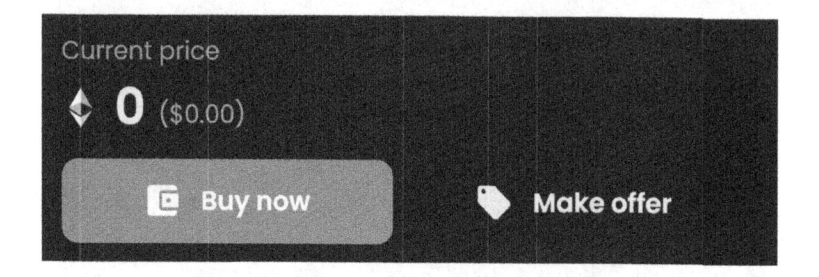

If it's a smaller, little-known collection without many sales or a verification sticker from Opensea, then you'll receive a gentle warning that the NFT you're about to buy is from an unreviewed collection. This will typically be fine, but it's used to help stop people from buying into a fake version (duplicate) of an original collection. Assuming you're going after a cheap one (as you should for your first), you will likely encounter this, so just check the "I understand" box and move forward, where it will show you a summary of the NFT's name, royalty fee, and price.

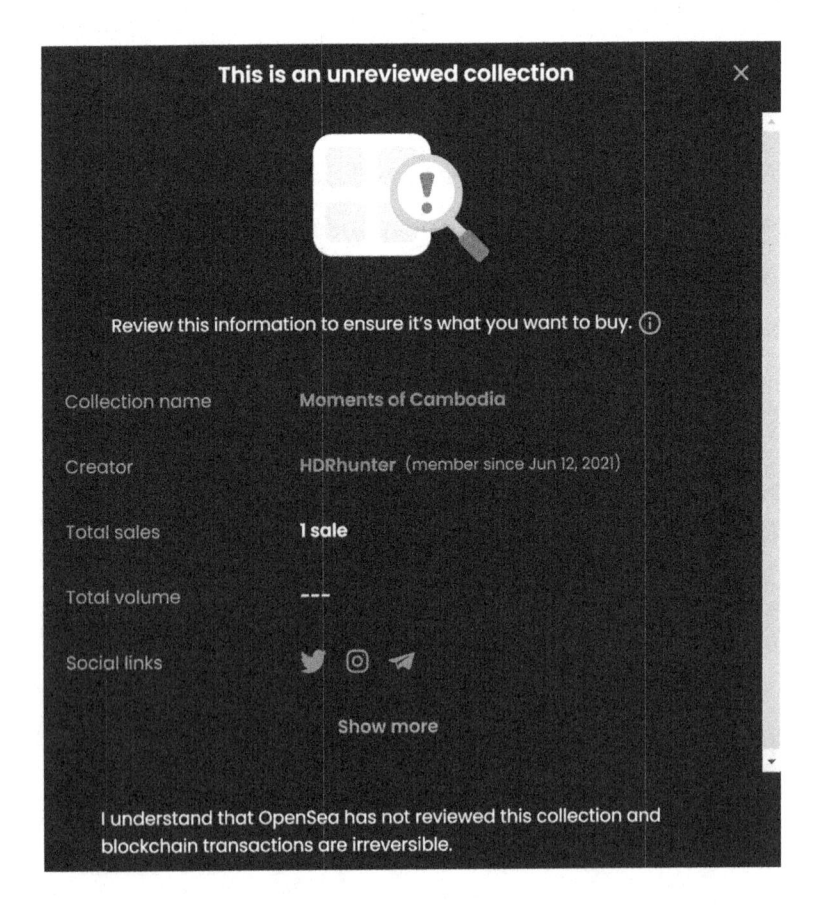

THE NFT EQUATION 103

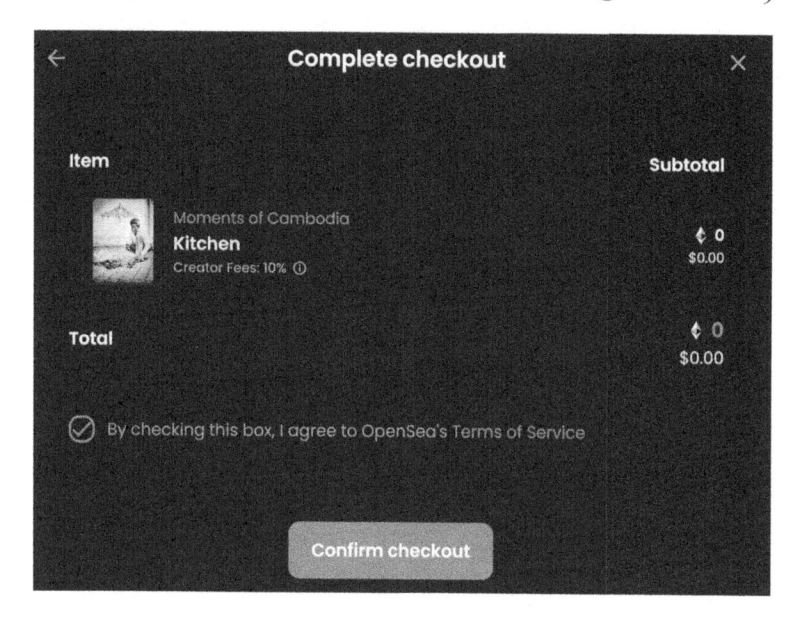

Make sure all looks good and click the checkbox to agree to Opensea's terms of service. The "confirm checkout" button will now be enabled, and once you click on it, your Metamask wallet will pop up asking you to pay a "gas fee."

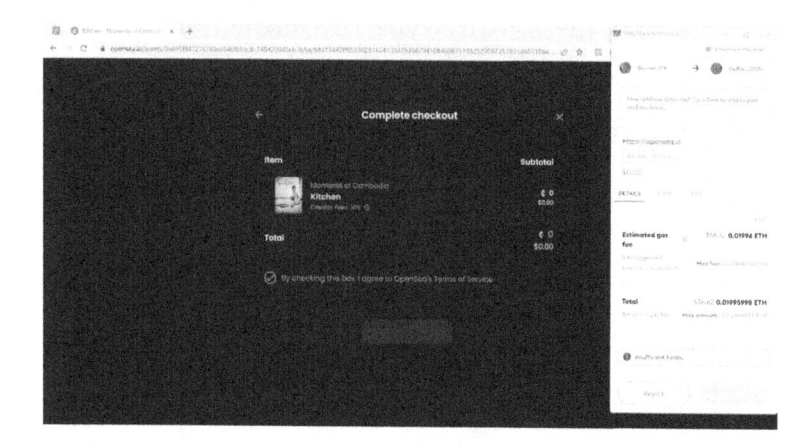

A gas fee for the Ethereum network/blockchain is similar to payment processor's fees like Paypal and Stripe have. It's essentially the cost of doing business on the Ethereum network. Like many other blockchains, each transaction submitted requires several confirmations or validations that verify its origin, amount, participants, and other data. These confirmations require computational power (mining) that miners need to be rewarded for. A key reason these gas fees exist is to pay miners to confirm our transactions and officially put them on the blockchain.

These gas fees can vary widely and depend on the type of transaction and the current traffic on the Ethereum blockchain. A transfer transaction, for example, typically won't be as data-rich (complex) as minting (creating) a new NFT for the first time, which would mean the transfer transaction would be cheaper than minting. The gas fee for any type of transaction will also depend heavily on how many people are currently trying to submit transactions on the blockchain at any given moment. If there's a big project launching where 30,000 people are trying to buy in/mint all at once, the gas fees can skyrocket to well over $500 (USD) worth of ETH in gas fees. Whereas, if the network is relatively quiet and slow, that gas fee could be $40 worth of ETH.

THE NFT EQUATION 105

The efficiency of the smart contracts (coding) behind an NFT will also play a significant role in gas fees, but that's a bit more of an advanced conversation.

Circling back to the purchasing step we're on now; you should see Metamask asking for a gas fee to be paid. I want to make clear that this gas fee is on top of what you're already paying for the NFT itself, so that total listed on Metamask now should have added up both prices. If you're ever unwilling to pay the gas fee because it's too high, you can always hit the "reject" option and wait for gas fees to be lower since they change by the minute. You do run the risk of someone else coming in and buying it, of course, so if you're really interested and ready to buy, go ahead and hit the confirm button.

If you're being told you don't have enough funds despite having more than the requested total amount on Metamask, look right below the total, and you'll see "max amount." Metamask essentially gives you a range of a gas fee that you'll have to pay, but they showcase their main estimate based on market conditions. Still, to submit a transaction, you'll need to have more than the "max amount," so you'll likely just need to top off your ETH balance to move forward with the purchase.

You may be tempted to click the "edit" button next to the estimated gas fee to save a few bucks. Don't get fancy now and try to do things your way. You get in there, and you're likely to fumble and actually lose the gas fee you paid but get no NFT because your transaction failed. Editing your gas fee can come at a later time once you have more experience. For now, accept the suggested gas fee. Within a few minutes, your transaction should be confirmed, and the NFT will be on its way to your wallet.

ALTERNATE STEP 3 - MAKING AN OFFER

Although I wouldn't recommend it for your first NFT purchase, there is the option to place a bid/offer on the NFT you want instead of buying it directly. When you place a bid, you actually won't pay the gas fee associated with a sell/transfer transaction that we just mentioned in the last step. Instead, if your bid is accepted, the seller will pay that gas fee themselves.

Now, why would you even place a bid in the first place? One reason is that there might not be a "buy now" button. This would mean the NFT isn't actually listed for sale at the moment. It may suggest that a past listing simply expired or the seller isn't currently interested in selling. Other times, there may be a buy now price that you simply don't agree with or cannot afford. In which case, making a bid would make sense.

Pro tip: if you notice that a seller keeps listing the NFT lower and lower over the course of a few days or hours, it probably means they are eager to get rid of it or need liquidity. These are prime opportunities to make a bid lower than what they're asking for with a good chance they'll accept just to get it over with.

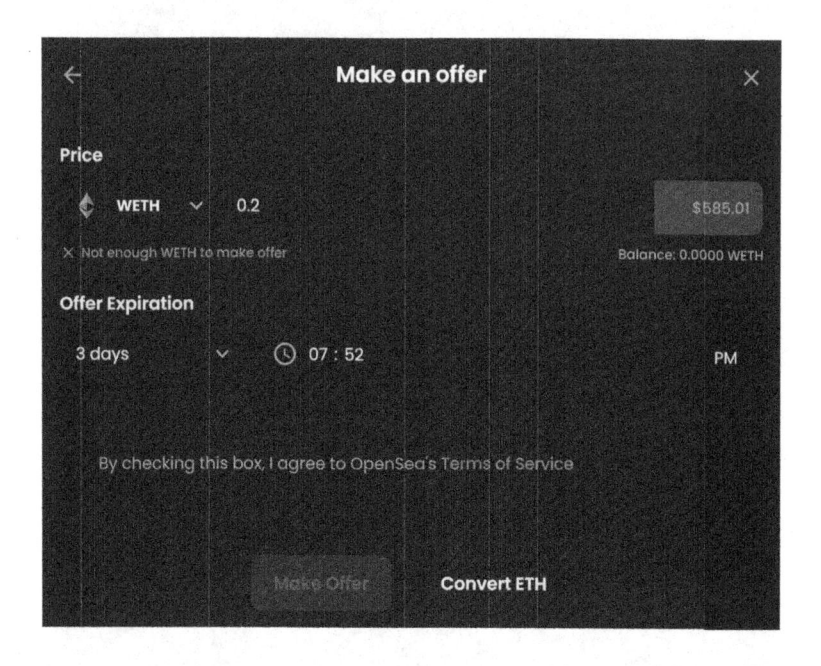

Make an offer

Price

WETH 0.2 $585.01

✗ Not enough WETH to make offer   Balance: 0.0000 WETH

Offer Expiration

3 days   ⏱ 07 : 52   PM

By checking this box, I agree to OpenSea's Terms of Service

Make Offer   **Convert ETH**

So, to place a bid, simply click "make offer" and input the amount of ETH you'd like to offer. Here, you'll notice that instead of saying "ETH," it actually says

"WETH," which stands for Wrapped Ether. Without getting technical, WETH is just a different type of ETH that we'll need to make offers. At this point, you don't have any WETH, so you'll need to swap your ETH to WETH in order to place a bid. The good news is, it's super simple, and it's a 1:1 ratio, so you won't miss out on much besides the gas fee to swap ETH to WETH.

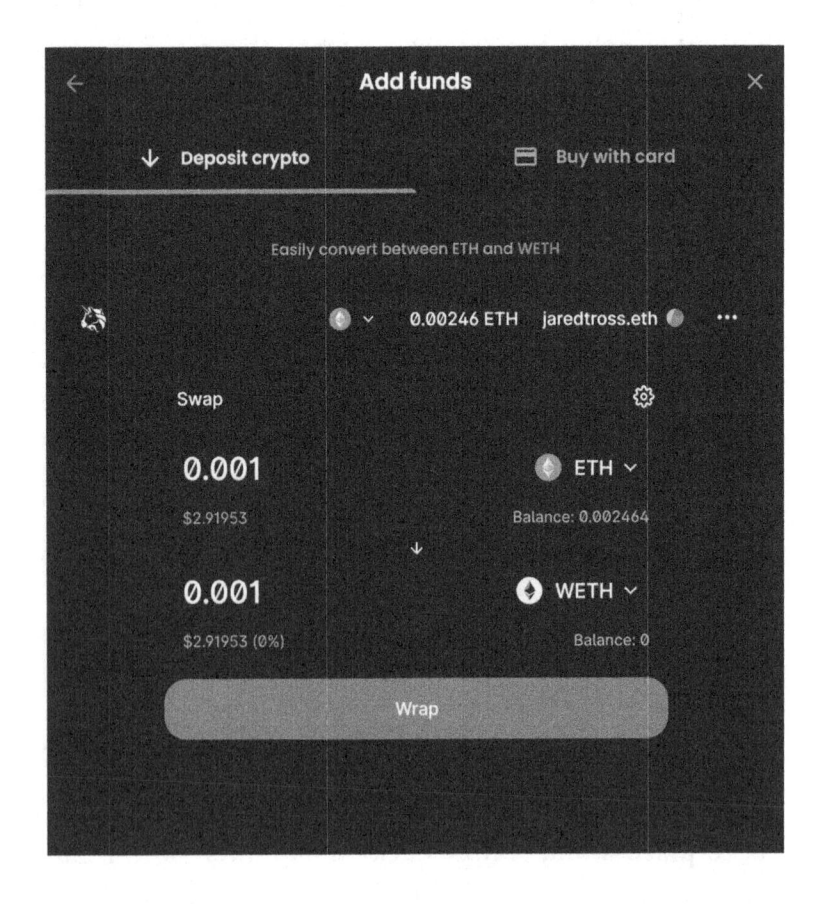

"Details" drop-down where you'll see the abbreviated contract address and token ID.

Copy and paste both of those into the appropriate fields and press import (because you need to copy and paste these, it's probably best to use a mobile browser to pull up Opensea so you can easily copy and paste and switch apps). Now, that NFT should be visible inside your Metamask, but just keep in mind that platforms like Opensea and Rarible are mostly display cases and marketplaces for your NFTs, and it's not where they're actually stored. If you ever want immutable proof of the location of your NFTs, you can visit etherscan.io and enter your wallet address to see everything inside your wallet. Etherscan is the blockchain explorer for the Ethereum blockchain that allows you to sift through everything going on with this particular blockchain.

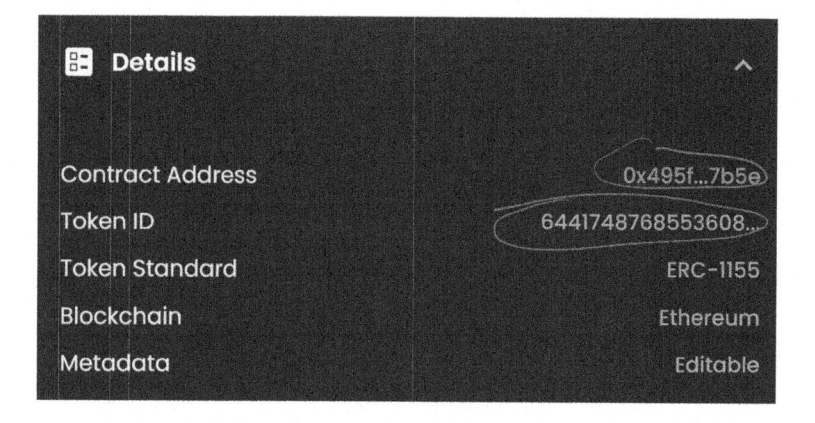

Details	
Contract Address	0x495f...7b5e
Token ID	6441748768553608...
Token Standard	ERC-1155
Blockchain	Ethereum
Metadata	Editable

Anyways, you should be good to go now, so congratulations...you have purchased your first NFT!

6

HOW TO CREATE YOUR FIRST NFT WITH NO TECHNICAL SKILLS

Here we are finally at the point where you can create your very own NFT! Since you're already set up with a wallet, some ETH, and have your Opensea and Rarible accounts situated, you're pretty much ready to get right into it. If you don't have all those things set up, go back and do it now if you're planning on executing as you read this book. If not, you can always come back later and follow along.

I want to make a very clear distinction before we move forward. Many people will talk about "creating" an NFT, but what they're really talking about is "designing" an NFT. Designing an NFT is the actual graphic design (or photography or videography, etc.) or visual element that will become an NFT. But the actual "creation" of an NFT refers to taking that digital asset and officially "minting" it onto the blockchain as an NFT. This creation, or minting, process means connecting a smart contract (the coding behind the scenes of an NFT) to the digital asset, which officially puts it on the blockchain. So make sure you have a clear distinction between those because this book will not teach you how to do graphic design. And keep in mind that there's not really such a thing as an "NFT design" or an "NFT designer"...there are just designs or visuals that can be turned into an NFT (which anything can).

Before I give you the steps for creating your own NFT, I'll suggest the same thing as I did in the last chapter: do not go through this process with profit intention on your first go-around. Focus on familiarizing yourself with the steps, and then you can do it with the intent to actually sell later on.

CREATING / MINTING AN NFT ON RARIBLE

First, we'll walk through the process on the Rarible marketplace. If you can manage listing something on eBay or Facebook Marketplace, you'll be in good shape to nail this process as you basically just fill in the blanks.

Step 1 - Choose Your Blockchain & Type

Once you're logged into Rarible with your wallet, hit the "Create" button in the top right of the page, and you'll be greeted with a screen that asks you to choose the blockchain you want to mint on. There are a couple of options, but let's not get confused for the time being and stick with the classic Ethereum blockchain.

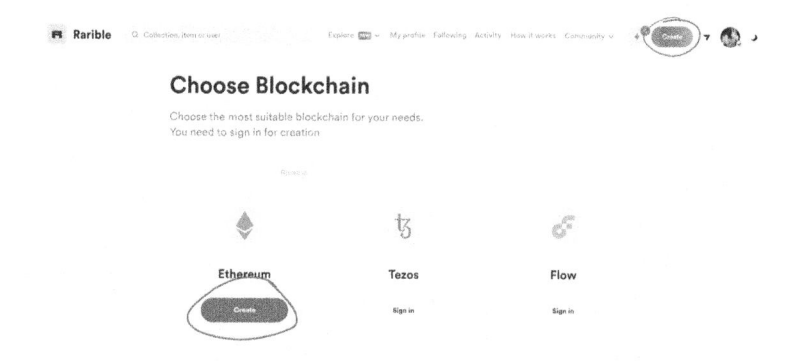

Next, you'll be asked to choose a "type" between Single and Multiple. Choose "Single" for one of a kind or "Multiple" if you want to sell one collectible multiple times. Totally up to you, but in this case, just follow along and select "multiple." This means I'll be turning one visual asset into multiple NFTs. This might work if I wanted to create some type of membership card NFT where I wanted 100 copies of the membership card to exist.

Choose Type

Choose "Single" for one of a kind or "Multiple" if you want to sell one collectible multiple times

Single
If you want to highlight the uniqueness and individuality of your item

Multiple
If you want to share your item with a large number of community members

Step 2 - Fill In The Blanks

Time for the heavy lifting, if you could call it that. On this page, you'll essentially be filling in the blanks to give Rarible all the info it needs to handle the behind-the-scenes elements of minting an NFT. I'll list out all of the different options you need to address on this page with explanations of each.

Upload file

First up, you need to select a digital file to upload that will become the NFT. As of now, Rarible lists PNG, GIF, WEBP, MP4, or MP3 as file options with a max file size of 100MB. So choose one of those file types from your computer and watch as it pops up onto the page.

Put on marketplace & Price

Having this feature turned on will mean that you want to list it for sale. If you turn it off, the NFT will be created and just sit inside your wallet. If you turn it on, then you'll have pricing options below, like opening it forbids or setting a fixed price. In this guide, let's just set a fixed price of 0.05 ETH.

You'll notice that you can choose some other currencies to accept as payment, but keep it simple and stick with ETH for now.

Unlock once purchased

The unlock once purchased, also called the unlockable content, is a feature that, when enabled, will give you a textbox to input additional material for NFT owners only. This text box can *only* be accessed by those who actively have the NFT inside their wallet. Some artists will use this feature to add a link to a google drive file where they uploaded behind the scenes video of them creating the art piece or an exclusive artist interview.

It's totally up to the creator and totally optional, but it's often a great way to integrate products or services into an NFT. For instance, I used the unlockable content feature when I turned an ebook into an NFT. The actual

NFT was just a 3D model of the book, but in order to get the PDF file to read, they had to open the unlockable content for the google drive link.

Choose collection

Choosing a collection is selecting a folder to put related NFTs inside of. If you plan to create several related NFTs down the line, it will make sense to choose to create your own, which will cost an additional gas fee. If you're just creating a single NFT (even if it has multiple copies like in our case), it will be more cost-effective to leave it in the broader ecosystem of the Rarible collection. It won't make that big of a difference, especially in our situation, so just leave the Rarible collection selected for now.

Free Minting

A relatively new feature on Rarible is this free minting option. Remember, minting (creating) an NFT will usually require a gas fee to be paid by the creator, but Rarible has implemented this feature to make it cheaper to create an NFT. Instead of eliminating the gas fee, it passes the fee on to the buyer.

I almost always recommend turning this feature off and paying that gas fee yourself as a courtesy to your customers. Unless you're making a massive collection of NFTs that all need to be individually minted, I believe you should be the one paying that gas fee for minting in most cases. So instead of burdening your buyer further, just take the hit yourself.

Name & Description

Pretty self-explanatory here. Just enter whatever you'd like to title the NFT and add a description that tells a bit about the design and ownership benefits.

Royalties

One of my favorite parts about NFTs for creators is the royalties!

Consider this scenario: A little-known painter sells a painting of hers for $100, a huge win for her at the time as she's just getting started in the world of painting. Fast forward two decades of consistently painting and growing her client base and audience, she's world-renowned and shown in art galleries in a dozen countries, with her paintings going for 6 and 7 figures regularly.

That buyer who supported her decades ago when they bought a painting of hers for $100 now has an asset they can sell for $1,000,000! So the buyer brings it to auction and pockets a million dollars after paying just $100 all those years ago.

In this scenario, the original artist gets absolutely nothing from that massive sale, but if that painting was turned into an NFT with a built-in royalty function, she would have received a percentage from that sale.

When you set a royalty percentage on an NFT, it means that the original creator will receive this percentage on every future secondary transaction that happens on that marketplace...forever. By default, Rarible will have this percentage set to 10%, which means you'd automatically be receiving 10% of the proceeds every time the NFT changes hands in the future. Of course, you get the total amount (minus Rarible fees) on initial sales, but as people buy and sell your NFT amongst themselves in the secondary market, you can be collecting royalties.

You can imagine if a superstar like Michael Jackson had an NFT. His NFT would likely still have a lucrative secondary market to this day, and his family estate could be collecting royalties right now. This is one of the reasons NFTs can be so powerful for artists; they can be rewarded for their work forever and even pass down those rewards (in the form of royalties) to their families long after they're gone.

Number of copies

Finally, you can enter the number of copies you want to create of this NFT. Remember, they'll all look the same, but each will have its own unique identifying ID code to distinguish them from each other. For example, I created about 100 copies of my ebook that I turned into an NFT. It means only 100 people can purchase the book directly from me before they have to go to the secondary market and find a past customer willing to sell if they want a copy.

Step 3 - Mint It

After filling out all those details, you can proceed by clicking the "create item" button at the bottom of the screen. When you hit this button, Rarible will take the information you input and plug it into a generic smart contract to create your NFT. Recall that a smart contract is the behind-the-scenes coding of an NFT that allows certain actions to be automatically executed once certain conditions are met, such as sending the NFT to a buyer or sending royalties to the creator's wallet.

Upon pressing create, Metamask should pop up and give you an estimated gas fee to pay to officially mint your NFT. Like always, if that fee is too high for your liking, you can reject it and come back later to see if the gas fee is more reasonable for you.

Once you pay that gas fee and your transaction is confirmed, you will have successfully created your very first NFT! No need to actually pay that gas fee if you're just doing this part for experience, but when you are serious about creating an NFT, then go ahead and pay that gas fee to get it on the blockchain officially!

As a reminder, I have a video tutorial that will guide you through this whole process at https://www.nftequation.com/bookbonus. You can also text me the word BONUS at 214-466-1640 and I'll send you the link directly!

CREATING / MINTING AN NFT ON OPENSEA

The process is only slightly different over on Opensea, so you'll know the basics of what to expect as we walk through this process.

Step 1 - Fill in The Blanks

Pressing the "create" button on the top right of Opensea will take you directly to the page where you can insert the information you need for your NFT. So now we can just walk through the process section by section.

As a side note, Opensea, by default, doesn't offer the option to mint multiple copies of an NFT, but they explain in their help section that you can enable this feature by adding "?enable_supply=true" to the end of the URL so that the full URL reads "https://opensea.io/asset/create?enable_supply=true" (without the quotation marks, of course). Why they made it this way instead of offering it by default... I'm not sure, but the option is there if you'd like. I'll move forward like it was always there in this tutorial.

Image, Video, Audio, or 3D Model

This is where you upload the file you want to turn into an NFT. Opensea does offer quite a few more options than Rarible does, including JPG, PNG, GIF, SVG, MP4, WEBM, MP3, WAV, OGG, GLB, GLTF, but also with a max file size of 100MB.

Name

I think you got this part down now. Give that NFT a name.

External link

If your NFT is connected or related to a particular website or platform, this is the place to link it. For example, if you wanted to create that membership card NFT we mentioned earlier, this would be a place to link a website that thoroughly explains the memberships details, benefits, and limitations instead of trying to pack all this into the description.

Description

You know how this part works as well. Talk about the visual, talk about the origins, and anything else you feel pertinent to include.

Collection

Same idea as on Rarible, but if you want to add the NFT to a collection here on Opensea, you'll need to have already created it before you got to this page. You can do this by hovering over your profile picture, clicking "my collections," hitting the create button there, and following those steps. It's inside the collection creation process where you'll be able to add royalty percentages as well, so make sure you go ahead and create a collection if you plan on using Opensea.

Properties, Levels, Stats

These are some settings you actually could have accessed over on Rarible if we had clicked on the "advanced settings" option while going through that, but it's not vital to the process we're going through right now. These settings are best used when creating a collection of different NFTs that will have varying degrees of rarity or access associated with them. They essentially help you create tiers of NFTs. For instance, if we wanted to have multiple membership levels for that membership card NFT, we could add a property for one NFT to be "Diamond" and then go through this process all over again but add a "Gold" or "Silver" property the next time around.

You probably don't need to get into those settings at this stage.

Unlockable Content

Once again, turning this on will give you a textbox to input additional material for NFT owners only. This textbox can *only* be accessed by those who actively have the NFT inside their wallet. Some artists will use this feature to add a link to a google drive file where they uploaded behind the scenes video of them creating the art piece or an exclusive artist interview.

Supply

Since we added that extra part of the URL, we should have the "supply" feature enabled that is the same as Rarible's "number of copies" option. Simply input however many copies of this NFT you want to be created.

Blockchain

Right now, Opensea only supports Ethereum and Polygon blockchains. Polygon is great because it is gas-free by nature! However, I personally don't care for NFTs based on Polygon unless there is a good reason for it because Ethereum based NFTs are more widely perceived as premium and less spammy.

Think about it; if there are no gas fees on Polygon, it means that scammers and spammers can have a great time creating fake or low-quality NFTs without a big investment like they'd need to do on the Ethereum blockchain. You'll learn more and likely warm up a bit to Polygon NFTs as you spend more time in this space, but for now, keep it selected on Ethereum.

By the way, at the time of this writing, Opensea is working on implementing the Solana blockchain into their platform, which will be a massive moment for that blockchain which is typically considered Ethereum's number one blockchain competitor for the NFT market.

Step 2 - Mint It

At the bottom, you'll see that precious "create" button, and once you press it, your NFT will be created. There is no need to pay a gas fee right away, but if you want to list it for sale, you will need to pay a wallet "initialization" gas fee on Opensea that enables your wallet to sell.

This fee can be pretty high, but you'll only need to pay it once per wallet.

LAZY MINTING VS CUSTOM SMART CONTRACTS

Now, I must explain something about the process we just went through. What you just did is referred to as "lazy minting." Lazy minting is just that: an easy way to create an NFT without getting into the nitty-gritty smart contract creation process.

This lazy minting process is great for beginners, one of one NFTs, or small-scale collections. However, when you see massive projects like the Bored Ape Yacht Club, you need to realize that they did not go through this process.

If you're aiming to operate anywhere close to that scale (having hundreds or thousands of unique NFTs), then the lazy minting process is not for you. Projects operating at that scale will hire a team of smart contract developers to build them a custom smart contract that gives them great customization, control, and ownership and then manually deploy that to the blockchain.

If this is a route you want to take, I highly recommend you hire multiple smart contract developers so they can keep an eye on each other's work for efficiency and integrity. If you only hire one in an effort to save money, you assume a greater risk of the dev making a bad smart contract or even putting malicious code inside that funnels funds away from you and into their wallet in the form of royalties. Therefore, hire multiple devs and ideally make sure they don't know each other unless they work within the same agency with a good reputation.

Where you find developers will vary widely, but you can study other successful projects and reach out to their devs via Discord or Twitter, do a google search, LinkedIn, or even find one on a freelancing platform like Upwork. You must be very cautious with the developers you hire!

7
THE INVESTOR'S APPROACH

Although I believe it's essential to understand the NFT space from both a buyer and seller perspective, I know that not everyone will be particularly interested in creating an NFT, so the following two chapters will be designed for those highly interested in investing in NFTs.

First, understand that just like businesses, most NFTs will absolutely fail and become worthless. Just because something is an NFT does not mean you should buy it or that it has any value. These upcoming two chapters will be primarily dialed in on finding NFT projects that may provide great benefits or significant profits, but the information will mostly not apply to projects tied to artists and designers who are selling one of one pieces of their artwork. Even then, the set of criteria I'm about to lay out will always have exceptions, but most people need to have some type of lens to look at the space through and analyze projects so you don't jump into any and everything. As you grow and mature in the space, you'll start to garner some discernment of your own. But for now, refer to this section of the book for some general guidelines in your search for the right NFTs.

*We talked about "minting," meaning the actual creation of an NFT earlier, but the term can also refer to when you buy into a project during its launch. Remember that minting an NFT does cost a gas fee, and if a project is launching thousands of NFTs in its collection, it wouldn't be reasonable for them to pay hundreds of thousands of dollars at launch to mint each of them. So although they are the creators, you'll be the one actually paying to mint the NFTs at launch, which will usually take place on their own custom-built website. I bring this up to offer clarity as we continue in this section.

FINDING NFT PROJECTS

One of the biggest questions beginners have in the space is, "How do I even find these NFT projects in the first place?!" The answer will vary widely, but I'll outline some of the top ways I find them.

Twitter

You might not like it, but you're going to have to spend lots of time on Twitter to find some juicy projects. After all, Twitter is the primary marketing vehicle for most good NFT projects. You'll need to follow particular hashtags and particular people to get your eyes on the right stuff, and you'll end up turning on post notifications for tons and tons of upcoming projects.

To help get your Twitter algorithm focused on the good stuff, I recommend following these accounts:

- @jaredtross of course (also be sure to follow me on Instagram by the same username)
- @zssbecker
- @jrnycrypto
- @elliotrades
- @NFTLlama
- @BAYC2745

You'll find many more fantastic accounts along the way, so follow success and learn from them as they'll often share what projects they have their eyes on.

*You'll find tons of projects being talked about and promoted on big NFT pages on Instagram. Unless you know and trust the source talking about those projects, they're probably complete shit and not worth your time (and are usually paid promos). Tons of dishonest marketing happens there by NFT projects as well. Suppose I see a generative NFT project running paid ads on Instagram talking about big celebs or having the best utility ever. In that case, it's usually a good sign to completely ignore it. Again, that's just a generalization and will not always be the case. Still, NFT projects that are low-quality or just scams will often target people on Instagram because people on Instagram tend to be less educated in the NFT world than Twitter.

Discord

You'll be joining a plethora of Discord communities over the coming weeks if you're not already deep inside at this point. Not all Discord servers are created equally, and you'll want to find the knowledgeable communities that are consistently sharing the elusive "alpha." In plain English, "alpha" is essentially an early heads-up about projects and opportunities in the NFT and crypto space.

Some of the best alpha discords that I'm in are my own (jaredtross.com/discord), Llamaverse, & Enigma Economy, but there are hundreds of others!

Noti Finance

This project is very much under the radar but very promising. I have spoken with one of the founders over zoom, and I bought into the project during its first launch (there will be more). In short, Noti Finance is a platform that allows you to easily track the smartest people's wallets in the NFT space and get alerted when they are buying, minting, or selling certain NFTs. They have tons of other features, but these alerts and wallet tracking are the primary ones. To access the platform, you can either pay a monthly fee or purchase a lifetime access NFT (I grabbed the NFT). There are other ways and platforms to track wallets, of course, but I personally haven't used something as fully featured as Noti Finance!

Visit www.noti.finance/jared to learn more about the platform and join their Discord.

*Update: Since I initially wrote this paragraph about Noti Finance, I've been invited to join their marketing board, so I am now involved more closely with the project.

NFT Calendars

Take this one with a grain of salt because most of the projects that end up on NFT calendars are usually low or mid-tier projects. A handful of platforms like Rarity Tools, NFTCatcher, and NFTCalendar allow projects to submit themselves to the platform and get featured on an upcoming NFT release calendar on their website. Plenty of the projects that end up there are legit, but plenty are low quality or scams. Exercise extreme caution finding NFTs here.

While this can be an option if you're struggling, make sure you thoroughly analyze projects found on these calendars to protect yourself. The best places to find projects will be from people and communities you trust via Discord and Twitter.

PROJECTS TO AVOID

There will be far more projects to steer clear of, so let's start with some of the top red flags (in my opinion) that you'll see in the space.

Lazy Art & Derivatives

This will be an element that's a challenge to have discernment about early in your journey, but after a few months, you'll start being able to recognize projects that put little to no effort into the artwork that was turned into the NFTs. Many projects will go to super cheap freelancing platforms and hire an artist to create a bunch of designs and call it a day. The more you see, the more you'll be able to identify artwork that was created by the same person for a different project. Personally, I want to see a high level of intentionality and effort go into a project's artwork.

It's also worth noting that there are artwork trends that happen in the NFT space at a macro scale that you'll need to be in the right circles to catch on to. One of those circles would be my Discord that you can join at jaredtross.com/discord (it's free, by the way). Sometimes the trend might be for pixelated projects (think Cryptopunks). Other times it will be for 3D, full-body NFT projects, or women-led projects. Whatever the current trend is, you should be aware of them because projects that are a part of that trend will likely experience pumps where there is a surge of sales volume that you can capitalize on.

Also under the umbrella of lazy art would be derivatives. After the massive success of the Bored Ape Yacht Club, there have been hundreds, if not thousands, of copycat or derivative projects that have come out that have their base character as an ape as well, just with a slightly different art style and different traits. Make no mistake, some derivative projects have also formed great communities and seen profits for their investors, but most are incredibly distasteful and short-lived.

Spammy Projects

Good luck avoiding spam projects in this world! Spammy projects will come in all shapes and sizes of spam, but one thing's for sure...we don't like spammy projects. A project can be considered spammy for a wide variety of reasons, but let's look at some of the most common.

Projects that encourage members (or have bots) to copy and paste mass direct messages to people inviting them to join or buy the project are almost always a no-go. They'll have bots, virtual assistants, or current community members reach out to completely random people on Twitter, Discord, and Instagram with a DM telling them all about the project and how it's about to "moon." I immediately delete these messages and write that project off as a P.O.S.

Other times, projects will conduct their spam in the comment section on Twitter and Instagram. Same idea as before, where they have their members or bots spam thousands of comments on random people's posts or tweets. Not a good look at all.

*There are some projects that coordinate Twitter "raids" where they ask their members to comment under a particular post by a big-name celebrity or influencer that has some relevance to them. This is different from telling members to spam a copy and paste message a hundred times. Raids are typically more strategic, tasteful, and not copy & paste spam.

Remember that the blockchain is open and transparent by nature, so we can look inside of other people's wallets and see what they've been up to. Often, newbies will find a big influencer such as Gary Vee and watch his wallet to see what he's buying or selling. Well, projects can actually mint NFTs directly to other people's wallets, and they'll do this to big name people like Gary Vee so that when new people check his wallet and see that he minted, or bought into, their project, they'll be inclined to click on it and do the same. Projects who do this are grimy and to be avoided at all costs. In later chapters, I'll offer some guidance on identifying real vs. fake mints.

I'll leave it at that for the spam projects, but you'll know 'em when you see 'em!

Overpromising Projects

Many projects promise their potential investors and communities the world without having any clear business plan or team who can execute. You should have a very skeptical perspective when hearing projects make big promises like passive income, 10 ETH floors, billionaire investors, etc.

When a project makes big promises, they need to have the team and plan that suggests they'll be able to execute it. Even then, I'll always prefer a project that underpromises and over-delivers.

Celebrity Investors

I've seen many projects blatantly lie about certain celebrities being invested in the project. I don't want to call them out (I'm pretty sure they've already failed, though), but one project was literally running paid advertisements saying that Kanye West bought into the project, which was not even remotely close to true. They'll lure you in with these big names and get you to buy in just because of the shock value of a big celeb having supposedly invested, but once you start asking for proof... they'll either ignore you or ban you from their discord community.

Sometimes, it will be legit that a big-name celeb has invested in the project, and that's great. Still, you should also be conscious of the fact that many celebrities or influencers could have been paid just to say that or actually bought in themselves but have no idea what they're doing.

Whitelist Grinders

You'll soon come across the concept of a "whitelist." If you aren't already familiar, a whitelist is just the presale list for an NFT project. You want to be on the whitelist so you can mint early and/or guarantee yourself an NFT from the project or even get into the project at a discount if they offer that.

So, how do you get on the illusive whitelist for a given project? Every single project will have different requirements for getting on the whitelist. But inside the NFT

Equation course, I teach the shortcuts that I personally use to get me on whitelists without always having to go through the criteria the project tells their community.

Some projects may offer whitelist spots for those who win them in some type of Twitter giveaway, fan art submissions, holders of other NFT projects, or a wide variety of other ways. But when I say "whitelist grinders," I'm referring to projects that require their members to spend all day on Discord inviting random people and leveling up inside their Discord. If you're new to Discord, it's just a chat platform for communities, and some discord "servers," AKA communities, will have a levels system where you can rank up depending on how many messages you send.

Projects that primarily give out whitelist spots to people who reach certain levels are essentially saying, "You can get whitelisted if you send X amount of messages." This is increasingly despised in the NFT space. Sometimes, the requirements will force you to stay on Discord sending messages (not random spam, but actually communicating with others) for 5+ hours a day just to get on the whitelist. This awful tactic is becoming extinct, but if you see a project doing this, it's usually a bad sign. It won't always keep me away from the project, but it is disappointing.

Short Term Planners

This is another one of those aspects that you will better be able to identify with time and experience, but many projects are very short-term planners. Right now, the NFT space is highly unregulated, but the hammer will come down from entities like the SEC and law firms in the near future, and many, many projects will be completely shut down because of their violations.

I know it may seem unfair that projects will get destroyed for violating rules that don't even exist yet, but that's precisely what will happen. However, the projects with smart teams that are long-term planners will be ready and have legal teams that have planned and anticipated what regulators are going to implement. These projects will be well-positioned for these future regulations, and if they do end up being in violation, they'll have the agility and flexibility built in to become compliant.

One of the most obvious areas that projects will crumble is in copyright violations. For whatever reason, people seem to think that copyright laws just don't apply to the NFT space. They think they can take a Disney character, turn it into an NFT, and profit all they want from it.

No sir. You might be able to get away with it at a small scale or until tighter regulation comes, but if you start having any degree of notoriety or success with a project that infringes on a copyright, you'll be in a great spot to get sued. Many projects will use the name, image, and likeness of famous people like Elon Musk or Jeff Bezos in their project and think there's no problem, but again, there are rules that could be violated.

I'm no attorney, so I'm not going to tell you specifically what's right or wrong, but I know there are many projects that are in the wrong and will be punished, so choose your projects carefully.

Now that we've covered some of the most common B.S. you'll see in projects, we'll take a look at how I analyze projects to identify strong fundamentals that indicate a project might be worth holding on to. I'll split the criteria into two separate parts, one for brand new or relatively new projects and another for projects that have already been released or established for a few months.

ANALYZING NEW PROJECT FUNDAMENTALS

The set of criteria we'll cover here is particularly relevant for projects that haven't launched yet or have just launched within a few weeks. Although this criteria is in the new project section, you'll still need to consider all of the following points when analyzing established projects. If you wonder where you find the answers to all the elements I'm going to cover, the answer will usually be a combination of the project's Discord server, their website, and possibly their whitepaper if they have one.

Team Transparency & History

Arguably the most important factor in determining a project's longevity will be the team driving it. The first thing I'm going to look for is whether or not the team is doxxed. The term doxxed means they are transparent with their real-life name, face, and identity. If a team is doxxed, it means their real reputation is tied to their project, and we can more easily hold them accountable if they try to scam us in any way. Having a doxxed team is always incredibly reassuring to me, but there will be plenty of situations where I make an exception to this if some of the other points are really strong. Ideally, we want a doxxed team whenever possible. After all, if they genuinely believe in their project, why not attach their reputation to it?

More than just being doxxed, I also want to see a team with relevant experience doing what they're doing. If there's a project team of 3 guys who are doxxed, but all they have experience doing is social media marketing and eCommerce... that's not really reassuring to me. In that case, the fact that they're doxxed destroys my confidence more than builds it. This exact scenario is all too common. You'll find a couple of eCommerce or marketing guys who know how to get people's attention online start a project, but they have just a few months of blockchain or NFT experience under their belt without much to show for it. They're opportunists, and part of me respects the hustle in them, but I typically won't want any part of the project unless there is a doxxed team with relevant experience with what they're doing.

The Jadu Hoverboard team, for example, is an AR company first and foremost. Their doxxed team has extensive history building in the augmented reality industry and the NFT world!

Roadmap

Next, I'll be analyzing a project's roadmap. Most projects will have a roadmap that outlines the project development milestones they plan to accomplish. Make no mistake; projects will use their roadmaps to deceive you into thinking it's better than it actually is.

When I look at a roadmap, I want to see true development, growth, and evolution of the project. However, most project roadmaps will instead be filled with cool moments in time. Items like giveaways, donations, merchandise, second collections, contests, marketing, or in-person or online events are all great things to have in a project, but they aren't true developments. True developments would mean actual growth of a project such as releasing an app, integration or development of games, launching their own cryptocurrency (they better have a team planning for SEC regulation if they do this), reinvestments into the community for some sort of business accelerator, DAO creation (this can sometimes be arbitrary though), or a variety of other developments.

I've seen some projects actually have two roadmaps: one for sales milestones where they do cool things like giveaways and donations and another that's actually for development. I like this approach quite a bit, but it's not necessary.

Anyways, what I want to see on a project's roadmap aside from true development, are items that are well-defined, actionable, exciting, and value-adding to holders. Determining these traits will be a challenge, but I will often form my opinion based on the team behind the project and ask myself if I believe they can execute what they've outlined.

I will say this: not every project needs to have some fantastic, unique, and exciting roadmap, and that's okay.

Community

The power of a project's community has a massive impact on floor prices and longevity. One of the first things I want to see is what kind of people are inside their Discord. Are the vast majority of members brand new to NFTs, incredibly confused, and thinking the project is "going to the moon" for no apparent reason? Or, is the community filled with people already involved in other successful projects and have reasonable expectations and genuine interest in the project? The main determining factor differentiating these two groups will be experience and education. Ultimately, you want to be in a community with people who have a high degree of education in the NFT space. Perhaps this education has come purely from experience and failures, or maybe they had a course like the NFT Equation to help guide them.

Either way, the conversations you see inside their Discord and on Twitter will give you a good indicator of what type of community is forming around the project.

On top of that, I want to see if the founding team is prioritizing community building or community nurturing. Every project knows how important it is to *build* a community, but too few focus on nurturing that community. Those projects that force whitelist grinds and invite contests as a means to get whitelisted will likely be those focused only on building a massive community. In contrast, projects offering free education and promoting conversations with depth and meaning will be those interested in community nurturing.

Utility

I'll start by saying that not every project needs to have a tremendous amount of utility or ownership benefit, but if that is what you're looking for (see the section of the book about buying objectives), then you need to raise the bar.

Lots of projects will tell you that their utility is access to in-person events or private masterminds (boy, do they love throwing out the private mastermind line), but those are only true utilities if the people in attendance at these events are high-value people you want to network with, or the "private mastermind" is being led by people who you actually care to learn from and not from the eCommerce founders behind the project itself. Don't let them trick you with some B.S. utility.

True utility is something like what Enigma Economy offers, where your NFT acts as a hash rate inside a cryptocurrency mining facility. This is a utility I only believed was genuinely going to happen because the team was doxxed, a detailed whitepaper & business plan was published, and a community of intelligent investors was formed early in this project's beginning.

And keep in mind that as the creator of an NFT, you can literally add an infinite amount of value by adding additional utilities at any point down the line. So project founders may say they give you XYZ utility now but add additional forms of utility in the future. This is another reason trusting the team is so important.

Novelty

The degree of novelty will also play a role in whether I see a project as fundamentally sound or not. It's definitely not the most important element, but you get tired of seeing the same old roadmaps and art style hundreds of times in this space.

Increasingly, I want to see a project that is trying to innovate or at least differentiate through the artwork, project structure, storyline/lore, ownership benefits, etc. Having an instinct for a project's novelty will only come after a lot of time researching and studying other projects, but it's well worth it to identify this trait in projects.

Supporters

Last but not least is considering who the supporters of the project are. I was hesitant to include this one because many new people can be deceived by seeing a big celeb or influencer say they like the project and automatically assume it's a good one to get into.

You must take this aspect with a grain of salt and recognize that people can be paid to promote the project. I personally use this to help me find worthwhile projects and avoid low-quality ones. If I see someone like Gary Vee, Elliotrades, or Alex Becker talk about a project, that's a very good sign! It doesn't mean I'll automatically get in it, but it does set off a trigger for me to go and look into it! However, if some rapper, who I can tell knows little to nothing about the NFT world and culture, starts posting about some new, small project, it's probably a good sign to stay away from it as it was likely a paid promo post. I'm tempted to call out some particular names that promote shitty projects, but I'll bite my tongue out of respect.

Just so you know, I've never done any paid promotions, and I don't plan on it. I will only ever promote projects I actually like and am interested in, and sometimes it may mean I'll be talking about a project I'm advising or consulting for. In the future, I may accept compensation in the form of NFTs, royalties, or whitelist spots for projects I am genuinely excited about, but I will never just accept upfront cash or crypto to promote a project I haven't researched or want to get involved in myself. Regardless, never let someone's interest in a project be the determining factor on whether you get into it or not, but do let it trigger you to check a project out.

Keep in mind that there are many more elements to consider than just these six, but these are the top-of-mind aspects I judge when looking at projects. Now, let's dive into a real example of how I used this set of criteria to find a winning project that we've already talked about: Enigma Economy.

Project Analysis Example: *Enigma Economy*

As a reminder, the Enigma Economy project launched their NFTs and used the funds raised from launch to build out a physical cryptocurrency mining facility that will allow NFT holders to earn a percentage of all earned crypto from the facility. I'll break down the Enigma Economy project from each of the six perspectives we just considered so you can get an idea of what it looks like when applied to an actual project all the way through.

Team Transparency & History

Right off the bat, it was a good sign that the majority of the team behind this project was doxxed (we were given their LinkedIn profiles via their discord server). More than that, however, the team had a history of professionalism and relevant experience in their roles. Whether it was cryptocurrency, development, or marketing, the team had the ingredients they needed to execute in each person's assigned areas. This built a lot of confidence and trust early on, which is very important in a project's infancy.

Roadmap

Interestingly enough, I spoke in the last section about how I want to see a more robust and exciting roadmap that emphasizes development. In the case of the Enigma Economy, the roadmap was pretty short and straightforward, which is perfectly fine in this instance due to the novelty and utility of the project. The roadmap they do have is very basic and to the point, and it summarized true development such as facility scaling, an ICO, and additional coins to be mined.

They've since updated their roadmap to have a few of those "cool moments" we spoke about earlier. Still, at the core, the roadmap doesn't need to be anything special when the whole point of the project is focused on mining, so as long as I see execution and scaling on that roadmap for this project, it's a good look to me.

Community

I noticed very early on in the project's inception that the community forming around it was really, really intelligent. I'd often discover that the people most interested were coming from half a decade or more of experience in the blockchain/cryptocurrency world and were intimately familiar with mining. The nature of this project's utility was almost certain to attract those with some context and experience because their whole premise is "mining," and most people don't even know what that is. It became abundantly clear that the people interested in this project knew what they were doing, which was a good sign.

On top of that, the community has started forming a trusted circle where we help each other find other great projects to get into and grab some profit. They've also been kind enough to share my free NFT Safety & Security Training with the community (free education). These are both excellent instances of community nurturing.

Utility

There's not too much to say on this front. There are not many utilities for the Enigma project besides the ability to earn passive crypto from the mining operation, but that alone is a powerful enough utility and having just that singular utility showcases the project's focus. You won't find utilities this great in most projects, and that's okay.

Novelty

It was apparent that this project's utility and value proposition were quite unique compared to most other projects, so there's not much to discuss here. The artwork is not something I'm a fan of, but the concept of the project overall was very attractive.

Far too many projects will make promises of "passive income" in their roadmap, and honestly, it's usually a red flag for me because they don't have the team or history in place to execute anything meaningful. And when most projects say "passive income," what they really mean is creating their own cryptocurrency and giving that to their holders passively. While that may be passive income in a sense, the coin is worthless unless the community becomes significant enough to the space as a whole and makes the value go up. On top of that, projects that create their own coin without planning for SEC regulation will likely be doomed. In contrast, the Enigma project is mining and distributing already existing cryptocurrencies like Ethereum.

Another aspect that made this project stand out to me was that they had a very professionally written whitepaper (business plan) that detailed the project's execution and financial projections. You don't see that often.

Supporters

I closely follow someone in this space named NFT Llama. He's got his own NFT project that I've bought into, his own discord community, a big Twitter presence, and he's someone whose opinion I value. So, when he started talking about the Enigma Economy project and did a livestream with them to further discuss their work, it was a clear indicator to me that I should check the project out.

Upon closer examination, I found all of what we just talked about and decided to buy in. This is another good instance of using the supporters of a project to prompt further research into it.

Results

So, I bought into the project during the launch at 0.07 ETH per NFT, and I bought three that are now worth about 0.5 ETH each! So that's a total of 0.21 turned into 1.5 ETH if I sold at the time of this writing. However, I'll be holding onto mine so I can earn passive rewards in crypto over the next few years. I even bought my fourth one a few months later for 0.15 ETH that's now worth double that!

At the time of this writing, the team is documenting the process of setting up the mining facility, and they've already shared the contracts they've signed with other companies to get things like their warehouse and GPU units for mining.

ANALYZING ESTABLISHED PROJECT FUNDAMENTALS

So, we just took a look at the criteria I use to judge projects that are brand new or mostly new. All of that should also be applied to evaluating established projects (in this case, we'll consider "established" to mean projects that aren't new or have been out for at least a month). But there are also some elements we should consider that are unique to established projects.

Again, all of these elements should be considered after you've considered the prior six we just discussed.

Ownership Percentage

When considering an already existing project to get into, one of the things I'll look at is the ownership percentage to see how widely distributed the collection is amongst its holders. Once you pull up a project's

Opensea collection page, you'll come across some data that looks like this:

9.6K	6.3K	2.26	13.8K
items	owners	floor price	volume traded

The number of items tells you how many total NFTs exist in the collection. The number of owners tells you the number of unique wallet addresses holding at least one of the NFTs from the collection. The floor price is the minimum "buy now" price at the moment. Volume traded lets you know how much ETH has been traded on the secondary market to buy NFTs from that particular collection.

When considering ownership percentages, we want to focus our attention on the first two data points; the number of items and the number of owners. What we want to see is a lot of unique owners compared to the number of items. In the example above, we would divide 6.3k by 9.6k and find that the ownership percentage is about 65% unique ownership. This is a very good ownership percentage for a project. It tells us that the NFTs in the project are pretty well distributed.

If we saw a project with 9.6k items and 9.5k owners, this would mean that almost ALL holders own just ONE NFT from the collection, and it's nearly 100% unique ownership. Conversely, if I saw a project with 9.6k items and 200 owners, that would indicate around a 2% ownership rate which is not great at all. Having too few people in control of the majority of the supply is risky because those few people could decide to leave the project and dump all their NFTs for dirt cheap prices and crash the project's floor value. On top of that, a wider distribution of NFTs means a larger, more robust community to help fuel its longevity.

Although there will always be exceptions, the closer to 100%, the better. One of those key exceptions would be projects that allow staking of NFTs. Staking an NFT is a feature some projects will have that will basically allow you to "pledge" or lock up your NFT to earn rewards. In the Enigma Economy project, for example, in order to earn your crypto rewards, you need to go to their site and stake your NFT. Staking will typically require actually sending the NFT to another wallet that the company/founding team controls. In most cases, you'll be able to easily unstake your NFT whenever you want if you'd like to sell it. When staking, your ownership is protected via the smart contract coding behind an NFT that will allow you to easily reclaim custody of the NFT without having to wait or trust that the team holding the NFT will send it back.

Anyways, when a project allows staking, all those staked NFTs will go to the same company wallet. This has the impact of artificially manipulating the unique owners shown on Opensea. If most NFTs are staked in the company wallet, then Opensea will show an incredibly low amount of unique owners, but in reality, the NFTs are just staked, and there could be a lot of unique owners.

If that confuses the hell out of you, good thing you're early in your journey and don't need to know that right now, but as you progress, this will make more sense.

Average Sale Price

Another factor for you to consider is the recent average sale price of NFTs within the project's collection. Remember that the floor price is the minimum "buy now" price the community of holders is willing to sell at. When looking at the average sale price of a collection, you'd ideally see it be well above the actual floor price.

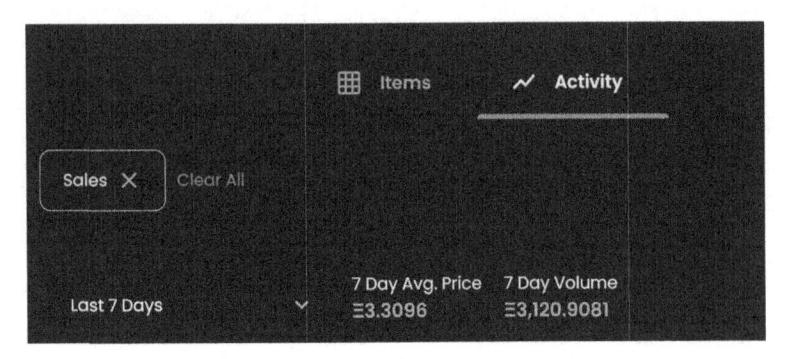

Sales ✕ Clear All	⊞ Items ⩘ **Activity**
Last 7 Days ⌄	7 Day Avg. Price 7 Day Volume Ξ3.3096 Ξ3,120.9081

When you see a recent average sale price well above the floor price, it shows that people who are investing are likely spending their time looking for a particular NFT they actually like instead of just buying in at the cheapest possible option (floor price). The more current, the more indicative, meaning the 7-day average price will be more relevant than the 90-day average price. While there are always exceptions, this tends to be a good ingredient for projects that may be worth holding onto or flipping.

Analyzing these criteria becomes less reliable and less meaningful when the project has experienced a recent pump in price or recent dump in price. It's most insightful during accumulation periods when the price is more stable.

Roadmap & Team Execution

This is by far one of the most important considerations to make when investing in an established project with long-term hold intentions. Ultimately, we put our faith in *teams* behind projects, and you want to get involved with a project with a team capable of following through on their promises.

Check their website and Discord to see what items on their roadmap have actually been executed and executed well. Again, donations, giveaways, contests, billboards/advertising, exclusive chats; they're all meaningless here because they're often exceedingly easy to accomplish. Find out what *true* developments they've followed through on or at least what they're close to finishing.

Also relevant in this category is team communication and professionalism. Have there been consistent updates inside their Discord? It certainly doesn't have to be daily updates, especially when a team executes at a high level. But generally, every 7-10 days *at least* would be a reasonable cadence for updates. The younger the project, the more important these frequent updates are. You don't want to be getting into a project whose team is unresponsive and uncommunicative.

Upcoming Developments

Aside from what the team has done, what are they planning to do? Jumping inside their Discord and finding out what developments are on the horizon is very important so you can do a pulse check to make sure the project has plans to continue to grow and expand.

Considering upcoming developments can be an indicator for you to get in for a quick flip or a long-term hold. If the development will be something loud and exciting but not that innovative or long-term oriented, it might be a good opportunity to flip. If the development truly is a long-term initiative that you believe will matter in 6 months to a year, it could be a good chance to get in a longer-term hold before getting priced out in the coming months.

You can typically find this upcoming development info inside their announcements channel in Discord or by asking the community in the general chat.

Discord Activity & Conversation

Before getting into an established project, it's a good idea to hang out inside their Discord for a couple of hours to get a sense of what the community is like and its viability. When I'm considering a project, I'll join their Discord and send a general message along the lines of "Hey, everyone just joined! I've been considering picking up a [insert NFT project name] on Opensea. When did you all get into this project, and what's your experience been so far?"

It's open-ended and straightforward, but the answers can be very telling. If the answers consist primarily of emojis and "do it bro, we're going to the moon any day now!" I'll probably sit that project to the side. When you have a handful of community members respond with thought-out, personal explanations of why they're enjoying the project, that's typically a good indicator of the culture the founding team has created and the type of people in the project.

You don't always have to actively engage, however. Sometimes I'll just join and occasionally check on the chat to see what the topic of conversation is and how often people are talking. If the last message sent in general chat was 4 hours ago, that's usually not a motivating sign for me, but if people are actively messaging each time I check the chat throughout the day, then I take a closer look. We also want to consider the substance of the conversation. A big red flag is if the floor price is the topic of conversation most of the time (unless it's during a big pump, then it makes sense). If the community is obsessing over how much they want the floor price to go up, then it doesn't make me very confident in the type of community members that are involved in the project.

Results

I bought into the Sappy Seals NFT project a few months ago for 0.5 ETH because of the analysis we just went over, and just two weeks ago, they had a pump to well over 2.5 ETH in their floor price. In fact, I was about to pull the trigger and sell the NFT I purchased and walk away with over 2 ETH in pure profit. However, the quality of the community changed my mind. In the heat of the pump, I analyzed some of these criteria for a second time, and I honestly had so much conviction in the project that I decided to hold onto my seal with the belief that a much higher floor will come in due time!

Since that 2.5+ ETH pump, the price has dipped back down to 1.26 ETH at the time of this writing. Still a great profit margin for me if I wanted to cash out, but instead, I will hold on because of the consistent execution from the team and the compassionate, funny, lighthearted community fueling the project.

While we just detailed the process I use to find projects with sound fundamentals that might be worth holding onto, what about making money on those projects that aren't so fundamentally sound but still have profit potential?

That's exactly what this next chapter will cover! Let's get into my favorite NFT flipping strategies that have netted me tens of thousands of dollars and brought consistent results for my students and me inside the NFT Equation course!

8

TOP NFT FLIPPING STRATEGIES

Coming from a student favorite in the NFT Equation curriculum are 3 of the top flipping strategies in the NFT space. I'll make this super easy to understand so you can participate in it yourself! Remember, if you're new to this space, flipping might be far too stressful and time-sensitive at the early stages. So don't feel obligated to do this, but it can certainly put you in great positions to have more liquidity to invest moving forward.

PRE-REVEAL FLIPPING

This is the strategy I used to consistently invest in projects risk-free! Before I break down the steps, let me build some context. Many of the generative NFT projects with thousands of different NFTs in their collection will have a placeholder image during the launch period until they finally reveal a day or two later. So what this means is that if a 10k NFT project sells out, all 10k NFTs have the exact same placeholder image, and no one knows which NFT they got or how rare it is. This pre-reveal stage is prime time to sell because there is a lot of excitement, uncertainty, and FOMO.

Step 1 - Identify Hype

The first thing you need to do is identify projects with a lot of hype pre-launch. You would find this hype between their Discord and Twitter presence, but you need to be cautious about fake hype and bots giving them inflated numbers. With experience, it becomes easier to filter out the B.S. hype vs the legit stuff.

If you see a project with 60k followers on Twitter and they regularly get 50-100 likes and a few dozen retweets on *most* of their posts and announcements, this imbalance of followers to engagement isn't very reassuring. It likely means they either have fake followers (sometimes their doing or sometimes targeted attacks or just unlucky), or the community has lost interest.

On the other hand, if that same project with 60k Twitter followers is regularly getting thousands of retweets and likes on even simple, non-announcement posts, that is a good sign! The Fishy Fam NFT project, for example, was one that I called clear as day as a great flipping opportunity. With 57k followers, they were regularly getting 2k+ likes and hundreds of retweets, not to mention all the comments they got! Even on a simple graphic post that said good morning, they received 600 retweets and around 3k likes.

Twitter alone usually won't be enough to confirm hype, however. You'll also want to join their Discord and see what that world is like. When searching for hype here, one of the first things I'll check is the announcement channel to see how many reactions each announcement post is getting. If it's a big discord with 30k+ people inside and I only see 100 reactions on the regular to announcements, that's not a good sign. I at least want to see a few hundred reactions for each announcement. On top of that, I'll check the main chat to see how frequently people are talking and how desperate they are to get on the whitelist (presale list).

Discernment in identifying hype is another one of those aspects that mostly comes with time and experience in the space, but I hope I've provided some basic guidelines on more objectively identifying it. Let's move on to the next step in this flipping strategy.

Step 2 - Get Whitelisted

The second step is getting yourself whitelisted for the project. Remember, getting on the whitelist is just getting on the presale list for the project. Each project's whitelist will have a different set of benefits, but they typically include discounted mint price and a guaranteed opportunity to mint if done within the presale time frame.

How you get on a project's whitelist will also vary from project to project, but they'll typically have that outlined inside their Discord. You may be tempted to rely on giveaways and random drawings to get on the whitelist, but luck is not a strategy. Inside the NFT Equation course, I teach my students extensively how I often color outside the lines of whitelist requirements to get myself noticed by the founding team and get whitelisted (by the way, it has nothing to do with my audience or reputation in the space). If you're interested in getting that training, then make sure to visit https://www.nftequation.com/enroll and enroll for in-depth video walkthroughs for everything you've read so far and much more!

How you get that whitelist spot will vary, but however you do it, it's vital for this flipping strategy to work consistently.

Step 3 - Buy Multiple

Once you've successfully gotten yourself on the whitelist and the launch day has come, you should be minting at least 2-3 NFTs from the project. We do this so we can flip some and hold others. Of course, not every project will even allow you to mint multiple. Some of the most popular projects will have a limit of just 1 NFT per wallet, whereas others may allow many more, so you'll have to adjust accordingly. If you're in a position where you can't afford to mint multiple, that's fine as well, but less than ideal. Again, aim for minting 3 NFTs from an overhyped project so you can flip some quickly and hold on to others for more profit potential.

Step 4 - Flip During Pre-Reveal

This step is where you cash out and become risk-free. As I mentioned, it is during this pre-reveal phase that there is the most hype and FOMO surrounding the project, and we want to take advantage of that fact. What you'll notice is that after the reveal has happened, almost every project will experience a big dip in floor price as people realize they didn't get a super rare one and want to move on to another project. This is precisely why we want to sell before the reveal.

Within minutes of minting your 3 NFTs, you should head over to Opensea and list one of your NFTs for sale immediately. The goal is to sell one of them for either the total cost of your initial investment or the current floor price, whichever is higher. If you do this successfully, you can safely hold on to the remaining 2 NFTs you purchased completely risk-free because you already covered your initial investment. If you can't get it listed immediately after you mint, then at least make sure you do so within the pre-reveal phase.

Pro-tip: When listing your NFT for sale, don't leave the duration for the default time period. Instead, change the date and time so that you only list it for 20-30 minutes. This way, your listing will automatically expire, and you won't have to pay a gas fee to delist it if you find that you need to set a lower price.

How you treat the remaining NFTs in your wallet will depend on your level of conviction in the project. If it's something you think is really only fueled by hype and won't have much longevity, then go ahead and sell them off as the floor price (hopefully) creeps higher. If you do have some level of conviction in them, then you may want to sell just one and hold onto your last one long-term and never have to worry about floor price because you're already in the green.

As a side note, you may have concerns that because it's during pre-reveal and no one knows how rare the NFT they got actually is, you may sell a super rare one as you're flipping. This is absolutely a risk, but you're playing the numbers game, and you're statistically very unlikely to get a rare NFT in a collection of 10k, so when you do this at scale, you're doing the right thing. Try to control that emotional part that fears you might sell a rare.

Pros

1. Of course, the most obvious pro is the potential to invest in a project risk-free. This is not a guarantee since it will depend highly on momentum and demand for the project. That's why it's so important to find projects with lots of pre-launch hype!
2. Another pro of this flipping strategy is the ability to quickly extract profits since we're utilizing all the excitement of a launch and the FOMO that accompanies it.
3. This strategy is designed to be emotion-free

(once you get over the fear of selling a rare, which, again, is statistically unlikely in most cases). Being able to trade and invest with little to no emotion is a huge asset which is one of the reasons I like this strategy.

Cons

1. The glaring potential con is selling a super rare NFT before you even knew it was a rare. Chances are slim, but when you execute this enough times, it will probably happen, and you have to be able to get over it.
2. Another potential con is missing out on even bigger floor pumps soon after you sell. It comes with the territory but investing is often more about minimizing risk than maximizing profit.
3. And of course, another con here is that there's a bigger upfront investment since you'll be buying multiple NFTs instead of just one.

Results

I could go on and on about how well this strategy works, but you can quickly look me up on Opensea and check the records. So instead, I'll highlight an instance where it saved me from getting scammed.

There's a type of scam called a rug pull. A rug pull is when a founding team launches a project and then abandons it altogether. Sometimes this will happen right after the project sells out, and then the team will delete their Discord and social media accounts and go ghost completely. Other times the team will sell out and do more of a soft, or slow, rug pull where they just make fewer and fewer updates and developments on the project and eventually go silent altogether.

I had never fallen victim to a rug pull scam until late January 2022, when the Blockverse project abandoned investors like myself. Without going into the details of their project, they were basically tying NFTs to upgradable Minecraft characters, and there was a lot of promise & hype for the project. Nonetheless, a few days after they sold out, they shut down shop and left investors in the dark.

Even when they rug pulled us all, I was still not a victim because of this flipping strategy! I minted 3 of the NFTs from the project, and I immediately flipped one to cover my initial investment for all three, so when they rug pulled and the floor price subsequently crashed, I still had 2 I was holding on to risk-free. So this strategy can, in some cases, make you immune to the rug pull scam. Use it wisely and consistently!

MOMENTUM FLIPPING

The Momentum Flipping strategy carries much more risk than the last one and is even more time-sensitive. When momentum flipping, we'll be using data to identify when an already existing project is having a big pump in sales volume, which usually precedes a pump in the floor price.

Step 1 - Identify A Sales Pump

The first step is knowing that something might be going on with a project. How you get your initial heads up on a potential sales pump will vary, but I usually hear about it from other Discord servers, Twitter, or by checking an NFT data analytics platform like Icy Tools. Remember, we're looking for a pump in the number of sales, not necessarily price right now.

Step 2 - Confirm With Data

Intimately tied with the first step, we now want to check multiple data sources to confirm that a project is pumping. You can use a few tools, including Opensea sales data under the "activity" tab, Icy Tools, or Nansen AI, to help give you insights on sales volume.

When checking a tool like Icy Tools, you'll want your eye on the 1 or 2-hour sales volume data, and I'm usually looking for at least 250+ in that time frame or 500+ within 24 hours. These are, of course, more arbitrary numbers than anything, but if you see ten sales a minute inside the Opensea activity tab, you might just have to pull the trigger and buy into that pump nice and early. Don't get too caught up in any numbers I throw out; it will always depend on the situation.

Step 3 - Rapid Research & Buy

Since these purchases typically won't be long-term holds, our standard due diligence and research should be expedited quite a bit. When I'm about to jump into a project for a momentum flip, my research into the project fundamentals will usually be 5-10 minutes because that's all I really have if I don't want to miss out. That research will usually consist of:

a) Finding out why the project is pumping in the first place by checking their Twitter & Discord.

b) Reading through their website to learn about the project's team and roadmap.

After your research, go ahead and buy 2-3 NFTs at the floor price, or you can go riskier and try to snipe rare ones (more on this inside the course).

Step 4 - Flip During The Pump

It's incredibly challenging to try to time the top of the pump, which is why I usually will sell one of the NFTs I picked up to cover my initial investment as soon as possible, then I can more comfortably ride out the pump. Often, I aim for no more than 3x-4x flips using this strategy.

If you're trying to get into a pump hours after it has started, it might be best to stay out. Don't try to chase pumps.

Pros

1. The first pro is the fact that this is a data-informed flip. In such an emotional space as the NFT world is, it's nice to be able to rely on data sometimes. Even then, it doesn't mean it's a bulletproof strategy.
2. The speed of this strategy can also be an asset as it allows you to quickly pull profits from the market as the opportunity becomes available to do so.

Cons

1. The top con has got to be the risk involved in this strategy. Without the experience, speed, and confidence, you're likely to get hurt doing this because you might join the pump too late or sell too late.
2. Just like the pre-reveal strategy, it is recommended to buy more than one NFT here, although it's less important for this strategy. If you choose to purchase multiple, the con is a more significant upfront investment compared to buying just one.

Results

A recent win I had using this strategy was with the 8sians project. This is all documented inside my free Discord, by the way, which you can join by visiting jaredtross.com/discord. I noticed the project was pumping by checking Icy Tools and seeing 700 sales in the last two hours, as well as people buzzing about it on Twitter. This pump played into a macro trend in the NFT space at the time of women-led projects having big run-ups. Anyways, I bought into the project at 0.15 and grabbed two NFTs at that price point.

I then flipped one of the NFTs I bought perfectly at the top of the pump at about 0.44 ETH. So yes, I turned 0.15 ETH into 0.44 ETH in a matter of hours (all this is visible in my Discord and on the blockchain,of course). I then held onto the remaining one for a few more days before selling it for a smaller profit.

LONG TERM / BLUE CHIP FLIPPING

We've covered some flipping strategies for projects we might not have full conviction in, but that doesn't mean we can't shave some profits off of some sure bets as well. This strategy is straightforward, but it will not be easy to execute (primarily because of emotion). The long-term hold flipping strategy is designed to be used on those projects you may consider to be "blue chips" (high-quality projects worth holding onto for years).

Step 1 - Strong Fundamentals

Since this is a strategy for our longer-term holds, after all, the first step is to identify a project with solid fundamentals that might make it a long-term hold. We covered the criteria I use in the previous chapter, but if you want more detailed analysis and examples, you can always find that in the course this book was based on. You also want there to be a decent amount of hype and FOMO around the project.

Step 2 - Get Whitelisted

As per usual, you want to get on that whitelist, so you have a chance to be a first-mover on the project.

Step 3 - Buy in FAST

As soon as that presale/whitelist mint begins, you want to be one of the first people to mint so you can be one of the first to sell. Ideally, you'll be buying 2-3 during launch, but many of these fundamentally sound projects with enough demand will only allow you to mint one, so do what you can.

Step 4 - Flip & Buy Back In

As soon as you've minted, head over to Opensea and sell 1 for as much as you can! Check the sales activity to see what they're selling for immediately. The best shot you have for maximizing will usually be in the first 10 minutes since you minted or when the project has sold out completely. If there's a pre-reveal phase, then you've got some more leeway, but if it's an instant reveal, the floor price is likely to start dipping pretty quick. Keep in mind that if you see the NFTs at the floor price getting snatched up almost instantly once they're listed, then it's a good indicator that you should probably list your NFT for a bit higher than the floor price so you can meet the secondary market where it's heading.

Assuming you only were able to mint one NFT from the collection and you sold it on the secondary, you now want to wait for the dip in price to happen. Dips are not guaranteed, but statistically, they're damn near sure to happen. If it's an instant reveal, wait a few hours or days for the dip to happen and buy back in for lower than the price you just sold for.

If there is a pre-reveal phase, wait until after the reveal when the floor price dips even harder and go shopping. After the reveal, you'll usually be able to buy back in at a lower price than what you sold for. So, you'd be walking away with essentially a risk-free investment in a potential blue-chip project, AND you get a little profit as well—kind of the best of both worlds, in my opinion.

Pros

1. The big pro in this strategy is the ability to take profits while still staying in a great long-term hold project.
2. As with the other strategies, you're still in a position to make very quick profits.
3. One of my favorite parts of this strategy is the ability to choose an NFT you personally like instead of just leaving it up to chance. You get this opportunity when you buy back in post reveal. I'll explain more when I go over my results using this strategy.

Cons

1. As usual, you run the risk of flipping a rare one, which could prove even more emotionally devastating in the case of a blue-chip project.
2. The floor could keep going up post-reveal and leave you priced out if you didn't profit enough

when you flipped during pre-reveal. This is incredibly unlikely and hasn't happened to me, but this is a concern.

3. This is a very emotional strategy because you're assuming that it's a blue-chip, and you run a big risk selling early with the anticipation of the floor dipping post reveal.

Results

My greatest win using this was with the Psychedelics Anonymous Genesis NFTs. Using the analysis we already covered, I was incredibly confident that this would prove to have blue-chip vibes, and I've been right thus far. I got on the whitelist (which was incredibly hard to get on) using the strategies I teach in the course, and I minted one of these NFTs for about 0.1 ETH, including gas fees.

Within the first two minutes, I rushed to Opensea and sold for 1.2 ETH! An easy 1 ETH+ flip within minutes, but it's interesting because the floor price within those first few minutes of the project launching was actually around 0.8 ETH, so how did I sell for that much? Part of it was luck, but part of it was watching the immediate sales activity. I noticed that the NFTs listed at that 0.8 price point were sold almost instantaneously. This means that by the time someone clicks on one of those NFTs at that price point, it's already sold. When you get this situation in the market, people will scroll down the listings and find NFTs that are priced higher because they'll at least be more likely to be available.

That's what happened in my case; someone scooped up my NFT pre-reveal for 1.2 ETH shortly after I posted. Now, as I said, this is a very emotional strategy, and I was personally terrified of the floor price climbing after the reveal, so within literal seconds of selling one for 1.2 ETH, I bought right back in at 0.8 ETH. So, I still walked away with about 0.2 ETH in pure profit and was therefore invested in the project risk-free, but I wasn't done flipping just yet.

A few days later (still in pre-reveal), I sold that NFT for 1.34 ETH, shaving off an additional 0.5 ETH in profit! Now I was terrified because I no longer held one of the Genesis NFTs, but I was counting on the high likelihood of the floor dipping post-reveal. Sure enough, a few hours into post-reveal, the floor price dipped, and I got to go shopping and choose an NFT from the collection I personally liked! I ended up buying slightly above the floor price to get Psychedelics Anonymous Genesis #2547 for 0.95 ETH!

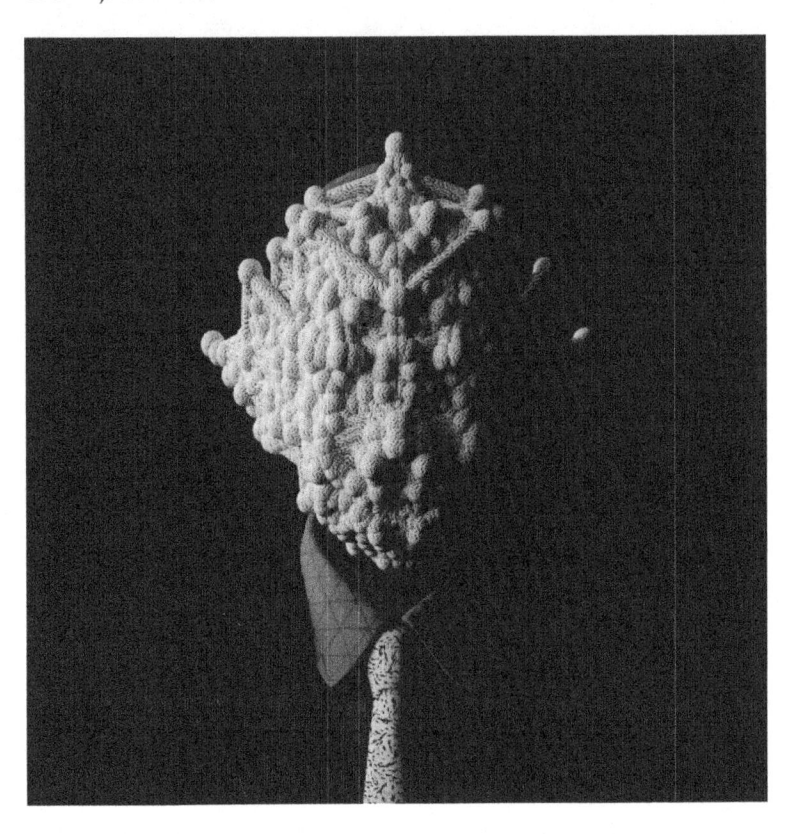

This was easily one of my greatest plays of flipping a blue-chip and still staying in the project (risk-free, by the way). I walked away with a risk-free asset that I genuinely liked *and* around 0.5 ETH in profit at the end of it all. That's how it's done!

9
THE CREATOR'S APPROACH

In this chapter, we'll look at the NFT space less from the investor side and more from the creator side to see how you can still make a profit in NFTs. Within the creator side, there are a couple of different angles to consider; the artist, the business owner, and the opportunist. None of them are particularly better than the other, and they'll each come with their own approach, but there are some fundamental elements they all have in common if you're to have the longevity of success in the space.

FUNDAMENTALS FOR NFT CREATORS

Remember that when I say "creator," it doesn't necessarily mean the person who created the visual element of the NFT. It's more so the person behind the NFT project or collection itself (the founder). This first section of the chapter will be focused on cementing some fundamentals for you to understand as an NFT creator that I believe you need to nail if you want to make it in whatever way you approach as a creator.

Integrity

I'm convinced that integrity will lead to the most success and wealth in the NFT space and the metaverse as a whole. There will absolutely be a ridiculous number of people operating with no integrity in space who end up making tons and tons of money. Don't be one of them. You might win in the short term, but never in the long run, so don't let the hype and FOMO lead you to act out of character and without integrity.

Take Your Time

I know that time is of the essence, especially in this space, but rushing through it will only hurt you; I can guarantee it. Before you even think about trying to sell NFTs, you need to spend dozens, if not hundreds, of hours studying this world first and foremost. On top of that, you should never be asking your audience to buy an NFT from you if you haven't even bought one yourself. That's like a lifelong vegan opening a butcher shop.

What the hell do they know about meat? You need to be intimately familiar with the customer journey you're asking your people to go through to buy your NFT. How else will you provide any customer service if they have questions or issues?

At the end of the day, you don't want to approach the NFT space with a get-rich-quick mindset. It just might happen, sure, but that's not what your intention should be if you want longevity and riches.

Build a Brand

Way too many people get into the NFT space thinking that just creating an NFT will be enough for people to want it. I've literally had someone message me a link to their Opensea listing of a painted leaf for sale for 2500 ETH or almost 8 Million dollars at the time. When I told them they were out of their damn mind, they rationalized it by saying it was "rare." This person had zero background or audience as an artist or NFT enthusiast. That demonstrated that they had a severe lack of understanding of what gives NFTs value. An item doesn't become valuable just because it's an NFT.

It's the brand and ownership benefits behind it that impact its value. A business doesn't suddenly have value just because an LLC is formed, and people know that, but seem to think an NFT just being an NFT will be worth something. NFTs are just like businesses, and most will utterly fail. If you want your NFTs to have longevity, you need to build a brand. Whether that brand is more around you and your artistry or more like a business, it doesn't matter. Projects and NFT creators with longevity will always build brands that communities can get behind.

Education

Education will be paramount both for your audience and yourself. The fact that you're reading this book is a good sign that you already value the education aspect of the NFT space, so I'll assume that you'll continue your education. More than just educating yourself, you need to make sure your audience is educated as well. Remember when we analyzed projects and one of the elements I considered was how educated the community members are?

When you have a highly educated community around your NFT project, not only will you keep them safer, but you're also more likely to build a stronger community that won't panic if the floor price doesn't 10x overnight or if there's a dip in the floor price. Ultimately, you want a super smart community, and how you build that education component will vary. Perhaps you'll start creating your own content for them to consume or compile other people's free content into a single location for your audience to learn from. Maybe you'll do giveaways of copies of this book or buy some community members a seat inside the NFT Equation course; I don't know. Jokes aside, make sure your community is safe and educated. One of the easiest ways to educate them on safety, in particular, is by sending them to my free NFT Safety & Security training that's taken right out of the NFT Equation course material. You can find that for free at https://www.nftequation.com/bookbonus.

NFTS FOR ARTISTS

I'll preface this section by saying that I am an artist myself. I do some acrylic painting, photography, videography, poetry, and know some basic graphic design. With that said, I have not turned my work into NFTs and tried selling it, and the reason why matters quite a bit if that's a route you want to take.

I didn't take that route with my art because that's not the brand I aim to build for myself. If I were serious about making it as an artist, then yes, I would be turning my work into NFTs after spending months or years branding myself as an artist!

If you're an artist of any art form and you want to get into NFTs, you need to show the world you're actually an artist instead of someone who may have artistic abilities just trying to make some quick money in the NFT world; like most supposed "artists." You won't effectively go from posting stupid selfies, food pics, and drunk videos on your Instagram and Twitter to telling all your followers about your new rare NFT available for 1 ETH on Opensea, but that's precisely what many attempt to do.

To speak from the investor perspective for a moment, when I'm buying a piece from an artist purely for the art, I actually want to know that I'm buying from someone who really does this work on a consistent basis and has been doing it long before NFTs came on their radar. There's an artist and fashion designer I've been following for years named Blu Boy, who has worked with global brands and hip hop superstars, who launched an NFT project of his own. I bought into it because I trust him as an artist, and I loved the work he turned into an NFT. If we look at the floor price at this moment, it's not doing too hot, but because I bought for the art and the artist behind it, I'm not pressed about it because I trust the artistry of Blu Boy since he's been doing what he's been doing for YEARS! In other words, he's created a brand and reputation as an artist while also refining his style right in front of his audience.

Remove this fantasy of busting into the NFT space with the artwork you just started doing three weeks ago and surpassing all the hardworking artists who've studied and marketed for years before you. Sure, it can absolutely happen that you blow up, and I do hope that happens for you, but if you come with that get-rich-quick mindset, you'll be climbing out on a very thin branch; it's just not sustainable.

My recommendation is that you begin building your audience around your art form first and foremost while you continue to study the NFT space and strategize how to best integrate your work with it. Once you've garnered some attention and kicked the idea of NFTs around with your community, maybe then start venturing into it.

NFTS FOR BUSINESS OWNERS

Remember that any and everything can be integrated into the world of NFTs (doesn't mean it always should, though). That means lines of business and products or services as well, so don't get caught up thinking you have to be an artist to get into the space.

I've had dozens of consultations with business owners where I helped them strategize on ways to integrate their existing products and services into NFTs. Someone came to me with a luxury car rental business, and we came up with the concept of creating an exclusive NFT luxury car club where the only people who could even rent (they still had to pay, but maybe at a cheaper rate) his luxury vehicles would be NFT owners. This adds a layer of exclusivity to an already exclusive business model (luxury vehicles). As we've discovered, some NFTs can absolutely be status symbols, and in this case, the NFT that serves as membership to the car club would be a status symbol with utility. That utility, of course, is access to the fleet of vehicles, and as that fleet grows to more cities and becomes more exotic, the value of that NFT would, in theory, increase as well. One of the clear benefits to holders (members) of the car club NFT would be the ability to resell it to someone else. Keep in mind that there are already car clubs that function similarly right now, but they don't use NFTs. Instead, if you're done with your membership (that you're probably paying monthly or yearly for, unlike with the NFT), you simply cancel it, and that's it. However, with the NFT version of this car club, you could resell it and walk away with a nice paycheck while someone else joins the club.

It can be a lot simpler in many other cases. Bring to mind that ebook of mine I mentioned earlier called the Crypto Audit Checklist. I offer this both as a regular ebook that you can pay for via credit or debit card and get the PDF emailed right to you, or you can buy the NFT edition that comes with lifetime updates. After purchasing the NFT edition, the NFT will go into your wallet, and you can access the unlockable content, which is the PDF file. In this instance, the NFT primarily functions as an alternative payment method as opposed to the car club example that creates more of a use case for the NFT integration into the business.

So, how do you integrate your line of business into NFTs? That's a challenge for me to answer without knowing your business model and systems myself. This is why it's critical that you spend the time to learn the NFT space because it is then that you will better be able to identify the best route to integrate NFTs into your business.

NFTS FOR THE OPPORTUNISTS

The word "opportunist" is sometimes a dirty word for those trying to take advantage of someone or something in a malicious way. That is not what I mean in this case. When I say "opportunist" in this context, I'm referring to the people who might not be artists or entrepreneurs already but truly see the value and power of NFTs and want to be involved. Often, these are the people who go on to create an entire project with thousands of NFTs inside of it.

I could write an entire book just about the process of designing, planning, and marketing an NFT project, and, in fact, I just might do that if I hear from enough of my readers that it's something they'd be interested in. Since this book is primarily for beginners who just need a solid foundational understanding of the NFT space, I won't spend much time walking you through the project creation process, but if that is something you're really interested in, then be sure to shoot me an email at hey@jaredtross.com or enroll in the NFT Equation course at www.nftequation.com/enroll where I do provide guidance in that department.

10

METAVERSE/NFT SAFETY & SECURITY

This is possibly the most important chapter to maintaining success and momentum in the NFT space. You can do everything else perfectly, but if you slip up on safety and security, all that hard work can be wiped away in seconds by scammers.

This is the wild, wild west, and scammers are thriving in this world because people aren't taught how to navigate it safely. I believe everyone deserves to be safe in the NFT and metaverse space which is why I took the safety and security module from the NFT Equation course and gave it away for free at https://www.nftequation.com/bookbonus. This chapter will summarize the contents of that training, but you should still give it a watch for yourself. Now, we'll cover the top scams and security risks in the NFT space, how to identify them, and how to protect yourself against these attacks.

MOST COMMON SCAMS

Airdropped NFTs

Remember how I said that it's safe to share your public wallet address? After all, people will need it to send you stuff, and they'll see it if you send them stuff. Well, yes, it is safe in and of itself, but what will eventually happen (whether you share your address or not actually) is you'll start to find a random NFT or two just pop up in your wallet. Normally, they'll automatically go to the "hidden" tab in your opensea profile, but sometimes not.

You might think it's a nice little surprise to find a free NFT just showing up, but this is not something you should interact with at all. There is debate on whether or not interacting with them really puts you at risk, but I've heard enough horror stories to be on the safer side. Basically, the concern is that the creator of these NFTs included malicious code in the smart contract of the NFT, and when you initiate a transaction (buy, list, sell, accept a bid, or transfer), they will have access to your wallet.

When one of these random NFTs pop into your wallet, the best thing to do is completely ignore it until Opensea eventually takes it down off their platform (it will still technically exist in your wallet though). You can also hit the "hide" option, which is not an actual interaction with the NFT.

Social Engineering

The age-old social engineering scam consists of the scammer mentally manipulating you into giving up sensitive information that creates an opportunity for them to obtain access to something they shouldn't. They may try to convince you to share information to help you troubleshoot an issue you're encountering or give you a promise of further success in the NFT space if you share private info. Always keep your guard up.

Discovered Seed Phrases

If someone gains access to your computer or phone physically or remotely and is able to explore saved files and notes, you're likely going to lose everything in your wallet if you have stored your seed phrase digitally. This is why it's essential that you write down your seed phrase on paper and store it safely. Any digital trace of it is at risk of being discovered by someone.

Fake Listings

As we learned, people can and will steal the visuals from NFTs and create fake versions. How can you tell when an NFT is a fake? Well, you should only be going to listings that are directly linked by the actual creator behind it. Going to a marketplace like Opensea and just typing in your favorite artist's name is a sure-fire way to come across fake listings. Instead, you should be referring to the creator's official Instagram, Twitter, or Discord to find official links to the collection or individual NFT.

Some other signs that a project is fake will be what blockchain it's on. Most scam & fake NFTs will be minted on the Polygon blockchain (purple ETH logo) because it's cheaper than the main ETH blockchain. Keep in mind that there are plenty of legit NFTs on Polygon, but scammers do like to hang out there, so be sure to know what blockchain the actual creator will be minting on.

Malicious Websites

As usual, there will be no shortage of malicious websites trying to scam you. You should exercise extreme caution when clicking on links from anyone! There will be plenty of projects and tools (like Metamask) that have impersonation sites created that look exactly like the original. You need to pay special attention to the URLs you visit before interacting with the site and connecting your wallet. Only click project links that are in the official Discord server or official Twitter account.

Hacked Discords

I know I just said only click links from the official Discord server, but you're likely to encounter a hacked Discord at one point. When a moderator or admin's account is compromised inside a Discord server, the scammer will try to scam all of the community members by sending out repetitive messages with a malicious link.

Usually, as soon as a scammer gains access to the Discord, they will have a templated message that says they are doing a "surprise" launch, and everyone should go mint right away. They'll include a scam link and spam the message dozens or hundreds of times to get people's immediate attention. No legit project will be spamming you a dozen times with a minting/buy link in the span of a few minutes.

Often, these situations will also mean that the scammers have disabled the chatrooms so members can't warn each other of the scam unfolding. Other times, the chat will still be available, and members will be able to help answer questions and warn others.

Impersonation

Projects, founders, and support teams of all kinds will be impersonated on every social media platform, so you need to be careful whom you're interacting with. If you get a random, unsolicited DM from a supposed "support team" member or a team member from a project, it's likely an impersonator trying to scam you.

These people are usually incredibly friendly and really act like they're trying to help you. They are not.

Giveaway DMs

At some point, you're going to receive a DM (on Discord, Twitter, Instagram, or another platform) that says you've won "0.4 BTC" or some other free crypto or NFT. You didn't win anything, and if you start clicking on the links they sent you, you're going to win an empty wallet.

Legit giveaways do happen all the time, but they will tell you how you'll be notified of being a winner, and you typically won't need to click any links. The best thing to do with these spam DMs about a giveaway you didn't even enter is to block and report them.

The Language Rope-A-Dope

Scammers will sometimes try to help you troubleshoot your Metamask or Opensea accounts by getting you to screen share and show them the problem. Not knowing any better, you might fall into this trap where they'll walk you through some troubleshooting steps over 20-30 minutes. Eventually, they'll ask you to go into your Metamask wallet settings and change your language to one they assume you don't know (often Arabic) so they can get you to click on sensitive info. They then guide you through your settings until they convince you to click a button (that you can't read because it's in a different language) that reveals your seed phrase or private keys, and at that point, it's game over for you since they were already screen recording.

If you're ever in a position where you're screen sharing during troubleshooting (you probably shouldn't be in that position anyway, by the way) and someone suggests changing your language...get out of there! If you've gone too far and revealed your info, get out of there ASAP and transfer all your assets to a brand new wallet on a different browser with a different seed phrase.

Rug Pulls

Ah, the classic rug pull scam. A team launches a project and rakes in thousands or millions of dollars before abandoning the project altogether and leaves investors out to dry. Rug pulls can happen quickly and by design, or they can be a soft rug pull where it's drawn out over weeks or months.

This is why it's essential to learn about and trust the team behind a project, and the anonymous nature of so many teams makes rug pulls pretty easy to pull off. You can protect yourself against that by using flipping strategies to secure your initial investment ASAP.

SECURITY STRATEGIES

Now that we've covered just a few of the most common scams in the NFT space, let's discuss the best ways to protect yourself from them.

Adjust Discord DM Settings

To help limit the amount of spam DMs you get on Discord, you can go into your settings and turn off DMs for everyone who isn't your friend on the platform. This is good practice because you'd otherwise be inundated by spammers and scammers trying to take advantage of you.

Record Seed Phrase on Paper

If you already have a crypto wallet whose seed phrase you created a digital copy of (whether typed or photographed), it's time to start a new wallet and only record the seed phrase on paper. Don't open yourself to more risk by having a digital version of your seed phrase.

Use Trusted Links

Once again, you should only click project-related links (like Opensea collection and minting links) provided directly from Discord admins, usually in their "official links" channel. There will be many honest community members who may give you the link, but this is not a time or place to blindly trust.

Lock Your Metamask

On the laptop version of Metamask (meaning browser extension), you can click on your Metamask profile icon and find a "lock" option. Typically, once you've entered your password into Metamask, it remains "unlocked" where your entire browser and any website can see and semi-access it. Of course, transactions will still have to be approved to be executed, and it's rare to have an issue with leaving it unlocked. Still, it's always a good idea to hit that lock button when you're not actively using it just as an extra layer of protection for you.

Create a Burner Wallet

You should absolutely have a burner wallet and a storage wallet. This burner wallet needs to be created on an entirely different browser or browser profile instead of opening your current Metamask and hitting the "create account" option. The reason you want an entirely new wallet is because you don't want the wallets operating under the same seed phrase.

Your burner wallet is what you should use to be minting projects directly from a website and interacting anywhere you aren't confident about safety. Your burner wallet should carry only enough crypto to carry out the transaction you're about to execute and nothing more. Another wallet should be used for storing valuable NFTs and larger amounts of crypto.

Get a Hard Wallet

There are hot wallets that are digital-only like your basic Metamask, and then there are hardware or cold wallets that essentially store your assets on a physical device. The assets stored on the hardware wallet are still vulnerable to market fluctuations, and you can still view them digitally, but the real benefit of keeping them on these types of wallets is that you can't complete a transaction unless you have the physical device in your hands and can click the buttons to approve it.

This makes it much more challenging for scammers because they either need to have tampered with your hardware wallet before it got to you, have the wallet in their own hands (and know your password for it), or have acquired your seed phrase. However, with a digital wallet only, they just need you to click on the wrong link, and they can get you.

Getting yourself a hardware wallet is non-negotiable, so get set up with one ASAP! The most popular recommendation you'll get is the Ledger Nano X, and I recommend it myself. To get your Ledger hardware wallet from the official site, you can use my affiliate link, jaredtross.com/ledger (which doesn't cost you anything extra). Don't waste your time if you're thinking about going bargain hunting for a hardware wallet from a third party. You should only ever buy hardware wallets directly from the official manufacturer, or you open yourself to the risk that the wallet was tampered with before it got to you.

Closing Remarks

As you can see, there is no shortage of vulnerabilities in the NFT space, but most of them are easily avoidable when you have the correct information. We only scratched the surface of what these scams might look like and how you can protect yourself. So I highly recommend you watch the free video training that this chapter is based on by visiting https://www.nftequation.com/bookbonus if you want to maximize the security you have in the NFT world.

CONCLUSION

Well, here we are, at the end of this book and the beginning (or next step) of your NFT journey. In this rapidly unfolding and evolving space, understand the tremendous risk you're about to engage in, but more importantly, try to have fun.

Keep in mind that this book was never designed to be all-encompassing of such an expansive space. You'd have to create a textbook to get significantly deeper, and the last thing a beginner needs is a big textbook to sift through before getting into an already confusing and intimidating space. Instead, this book should offer new people an excellent start in the world of NFTs.

I know that there will be people who are very knowledgeable in the NFT space who read this book and say,

"Well, you forgot about ____!" or "Why didn't you bring up ____?!" And the reality is, I couldn't fit everything I wanted to in this book and still keep it safe and digestible for beginners. That's precisely why I created the NFT Equation as a course as well.

The NFT Equation course is constantly evolving and updated as the NFT space and my knowledge grows and evolves. So, once you're a student in it, you get those lifetime updates at no cost, which means you get a lot more than what you pay for. Many online "courses" are really just big folders of live streams people have done talking about the topic at hand, but the NFT Equation is a highly structured and organized course that I've taught as a guest lecturer at the University level multiple times. If you're interested in further enhancing your knowledge and safety in the NFT space, I invite you to enroll in the NFT Equation course at www.nftequation.com/enroll. As a special thank you for reading this book, I'm happy to offer you 25% off the listed price using the code BOOK25 at checkout!

I invite you to stay in touch with me via Instagram (@jaredtross) or text me directly at 214-466-1640 whenever you have questions about NFTs or just want to talk.

To close, I want to remind you that just like most businesses fail, most NFTs will become worthless. This is why it's imperative that you have analysis criteria from an investor approach and that you are serious about building a project (business) of value from the creator side of things.

The future moves faster, and I hope this book helps you keep up.

P.S. As an author, the best way my readers can thank me for the book is by writing a stellar, honest review on Amazon. If you could take just 2-3 minutes out of your day to leave me a good rating, it would mean the world to me! Thank you!

You can visit nftequation.com/bookreview

Customer reviews

★★★★☆ 4.7 out of 5

141 global ratings

5 star		81%
4 star		10%
3 star		6%
2 star		2%
1 star		1%

Review this product

Share your thoughts with other customers

Write a customer review

⬅

How are ratings calculated?

SPECIAL THANKS

I'd like to give a special thank you to my girlfriend, Priscilla, who has supported my decision to retire from college and take a leap of faith. She has been there and loyal through times of uncertainty, stress, and shortcomings. Her patience is what has allowed me to obsess over this NFT world and figure out ways to help others navigate it.

I'd also like to thank global thought leader 19 Keys for the educational resources and guidance he offered me early in my journey into this space and his willingness to work with and believe in me before & after I found my footing.

REFERENCES

Bogan, V. (2021, March). *The greater fool theory: What is it?* Hartford Funds. Retrieved February 18, 2022, from https://www.hartfordfunds.com/insights/investor-insight/the-greater-fool-theory-what-is-it.html

Hayes, A. (2022, February 16). *Blockchain explained.* Investopedia. Retrieved February 15, 2022, from https://www.investopedia.com/terms/b/blockchain.asp

Versprille, A. (2022, January 6). *NFT Market Surpassed $40 Billion in 2021, New Estimate Shows.* Bloomberg.com. Retrieved February 15, 2022, from https://www.bloomberg.com/news/articles/2022-01-06/nft-market-surpassed-40-billion-in-2021-new-estimate-shows

Made in the USA
Coppell, TX
10 September 2022